ETHNIC CHRONOLOGY SERIES
NUMBER 10

The Irish in America 550-1972

A Chronology & Fact Book

Compiled and edited by
William D. Griffin

1973
OCEANA PUBLICATIONS, INC.
DOBBS FERRY, NEW YORK

Library of Congress Cataloging in Publication Data

Griffin, William D comp.
The Irish in America, 550-1972.

(Ethnic chronology series, no. 10)
Bibliography: p.
1. Irish in the United States--History--Chronology. 2. Irish in the United States--History--Sources. I. Title. II. Series.
E184.I6G74 301.45'19'162073 73-3405
ISBN 0-373-00501-8

Manufactured in the United States of America

TABLE OF CONTENTS

EDITOR'S FOREWORD

The Irish-Americans enjoy a unique distinction in this country of immigrants. There are now three times as many persons of Irish descent in the United States as there are in Ireland. In effect, the Irish Race has transferred itself, and its posterity, to America.

But just as no other immigrant group has physically forsaken the old country to such a degree, so no other has remained so spiritually attached to its homeland, or so committed to her interests. Given the extent and the complexity of the Irish experience in America, and the limitations of space and format, one cannot hope to do more in a chronology than touch upon some of the highlights and indicate some of the trends in that experience.

While no attempt has been made to include all the notable Irish-Americans of the past three centuries, a representative selection of those whose deeds illuminate the Irish role in America has been integrated into the chronology. A greater than usual emphasis upon the earlier, less-known period of Irish settlement has been balanced by a corresponding de-emphasis in certain well-publicized areas, such as sports and entertainment.

It is widely believed that the Irish did not begin coming to America in large numbers until the 1830's and that those who emigrated from Ireland at an earlier date all belonged to a breed designated "Scotch-Irish." There were, in fact, thousands of Irish Catholics residing in the United States by the beginning of the nineteenth century. There were also thousands of Irish Episcopalians, Methodists, Quakers and Baptists from all the provinces of the mother country. And, finally, there were tens of thousands of Irish Presbyterians, descended from seventeenth-century Scottish settlers in Ulster. All of these immigrants from Ireland and their progeny were known, without distinction, among themselves and by other Americans, as "Irish." It was only when the great mass of Catholic peasants from the southern provinces of the island began flowing into the

United States during the 1840's that old, established Irish-American families, desirous of avoiding identification with the unpopular newcomers, began calling themselves by the artificial appellation "Scotch-Irish," though many possessed no tincture of Scottish blood whatsoever, but merely adhered to one of the Protestant churches. In keeping with historical accuracy, this chronology follows the original practice of regarding all natives of Ireland as having common nationality, despite sectarian distinctions.

The Chronology aims at providing, in concise form, the major historical facts in the development of the Irish-American community. The statistical and documentary material in this book has been selected to illustrate and substantiate the story traced in the Chronology.

CHRONOLOGY

	Pre-Christian Irish legends repeatedly refer to "enchanted Islands to the West," lying far out in the Ocean--Tir na-Og, the "land of eternal youth," and Hy Brasil, the "island of great desire."
c.550	According to Irish tradition, St. Brendan the Navigator, sailing westward in search of new mission fields, reached inhabited lands and preached the Gospel to the natives.
c.670	Irish monks, pursuing their overseas missionary efforts, discovered the Faeroe Islands.
790	Irish monks, still moving westward in search of legendary inhabited islands, reached Iceland, from which they were ousted by the Vikings some sixty years later.
c.1000	Norse sagas refer to "Great Ireland," lying to the southwest of Greenland and inhabited at this period by "white-skinned people," descended from early Irish voyagers.
	Although such chroniclers as Dalerto(1325) and Fra Mauro (1459) continued to refer to Hy Brasil lying west of Ireland, no further evidence of contacts between medieval Ireland and America has been found to support these Gaelic and Norse traditions.
1492	Among Columbus' sailors was William Eris, or Ayers, a native of Galway, Ireland. He was one of the forty volunteers left behind on Hispaniola, who were killed by the Indians before Columbus' return.
1560-80	The Elizabethan "colonization" of Ireland by means of "plantations" among the native Celts were the forerunners of similar attempts during the 1580's by men who had gained experience in Ireland--Grenville, Gilbert, St. Leger, Raleigh,

Drake--to plant an English colony in America. Ireland was the training-ground and staging-area for England's transatlantic expansion.

1586 During Sir Richard Grenville's expedition to North America Captain Ralph Lane writes that "An Irishman serving me, one Edward Nugent volunteered to kill Pemisapan, King of the Indians. We met him returning out of the woods with Pemisapan's head in his hands, and the Indians ceased their raids against the English Camp." (near present-day Edenton, N. C.)

1587 During Captain John White's Fourth Voyage to Virginia "two Irishmen, Darbie Glaven and Dennis Carrell" were put ashore on St. John (Virgin Islands) to collect supplies and fill water barrels. For some unrecorded reason they were left behind when the ships sailed, and were heard of no more.

1607 Francis Maguire, an Irishman, came to Jamestown, Virginia, with Captain Newport, remained about one year. He subsequently wrote an account of his visit and submitted it to the Spanish Council of State.

1609 John Coleman, an Irish sailor on Henry Hudson's Half Moon, killed in a clash with Indians on the coast of New Jersey. The place where he died was named Coleman's Point, but is now known as Sandy Hook. Coleman was buried at Coney Island.

1621 The Flying Harte arrived at Newport News, Virginia, with a large party of Irish settlers led by Daniel Gookin, a wealthy Quaker merchant from Cork. (The town in Virginia supposedly takes its name from his birthplace, Port Newce, in County Cork.)

1625 The Due Return arrived at Jamestown in January, commanded by "Symon Turchin, who had been banished out of Ireland and was reported strongly affected to Popery." He was forced by the Governor of Virginia to sail back to England.

1635 John and Cornelius Sullivan are listed as settlers, in Virginia land records. The latter, possessed of considerable property, died in 1672, leaving legacies to his "countrymen" Patrick Norton and John Kelly.

1639 Alexander Bryan, from Armagh, settled at Milford, Connecticut. In 1661 he bought from the Indians the last 20 acres they owned in the district for "6 coats, 3 blankets and 3 pairs of breeches."

1640 Darby Field, an Irishman, was sent by Governor Winthrop of Massachusetts Bay Colony to explore northern New England.

He discovered the White Mountains.

Michael Bacon, from Dublin, settled in Boston and later received a grant of land in Woburn, Massachusetts. A descendant, John Bacon, was among the Minute Men killed at Lexington Green in 1775.

1644 Daniel Gookin, the Younger (1612-1687), son of an early Irish settler in Virginia, moved to Massachusetts where he became a member of the governor's council, Major General of militia and Superintendent of Indian affairs.

1645 Teague Jones (d. 1676), a native of Ireland, became a freeholder and resident of Yarmouth, Massachusetts. He was fined in 1660 for refusing to take oath of fidelity to the Crown.

Dutch colonial records list "Jan Andriessen de Iersman van Dublingh" (John Anderson, the Irishman from Dublin) as a resident at Beverwyck, near Fort Orange (Albany). He died in 1664, the year of New Amsterdam's capture by the British.

1652 Oliver Cromwell, victorious in his campaigns in Ireland, began large-scale confiscation of Irish land. Thousands of Irish men and women were dispossessed and many of them transported as laborers to the West Indies. Some of the transported Irish (especially those in Barbados) subsequently found their way to British colonies on the North American mainland.

1653 James Butler, a native of Ireland, settled in Massachusetts. At his death in 1681 he was the largest landowner in what is now Worcester, Massachusetts.

1657 Thomas Lewis, from Belfast, arrived in New Amsterdam as a carpenter under contract to the Dutch West India Company. Under the name of Thomas Lodewicksen he became captain of a cargo vessel plying the Hudson River between New Amsterdam and Fort Orange (Albany). He was a special protegé of Governor Stuyvesant and is mentioned in Stuyvesant's correspondence as Thomas the Irishman. He died in 1685 leaving a son, Thomas, who married the daughter of Governor Leisler.

1662 Town of Kinsale founded in Virginia by Irish settlers from Cork.

1669 Michael Kelly, a native of Ireland, commissioned by the Council of Rhode Island to prepare defensive works against Indian attacks.

1670 English and Irish emigrants established a settlement at Charleston and begin the colonization of South Carolina. One of the ships in the first fleet was commanded by Capt. Florence O'Sullivan, who was named Surveyor-General of the new province and commander of the militia. Sullivan's Island in Charleston harbor is named after him.

1672 Robert Pollock from Donegal and his wife (a native of Londonderry) arrived in Maryland. Their son William, who contracted the name to Polk, was the great-grandfather of President James K. Polk.

1677 Charles McCarthy, from Cork, led a party of 48 Irish emigrants in the founding of East Greenwich, Rhode Island.

1678 About 100 Irish families sailed from Barbados to Virginia and the Carolinas.

1680 George Talbot "an Irish gentleman" received a land grant in Maryland which he named New Ireland, and subdivided into estates called New Munster, New Leinster, and New Connaught. It included what is now Hartford and Cecil Counties, Maryland and part of Newcastle County, Delaware, and was settled by Irish immigrants.

1682 Dennis and Mary Rochford from Wexford accompanied William Penn on his first visit to Pennsylvania. Dennis was named a member of the Pennsylvania Assembly in 1683.

Sir Thomas Dongan (1634-1715), born in Kildare, named Governor of New York. He held the post until 1688 and was subsequently created Earl of Limerick.

1683 Irish immigrants from Tipperary settled in Salem County, New Jersey.

1684 Richard Kryle, "an Irish gentleman", named Governor of South Carolina. During his term there was a considerable influx of Irish settlers.

1685 James Moore (1640-1703), a native of Ireland, appointed a member of the Carolina Council. He subsequently served as acting governor, Chief Justice of the province, and Attorney General. His son James became governor of South Carolina in 1719.

1688 Anne Glover hanged as a witch in Boston. A native of Ireland, she had been sold as a slave in Barbados in Cromwell's time and subsequently brought to Massachusetts.

Charles Carroll was named Attorney General of Maryland by Lord Calvert, the Proprietor. He was the grandfather of Charles Carroll of Carrollton, a signer of the Declaration of Independence, and was the founder of one of the most distinguished and prosperous Irish-American families of the colonial era.

1690 Andrew Meade, from Kerry, settled in Nansemond County, Virginia, and later became a Burgess, a Judge and a Colonel of militia. Among his descendants was General George Meade, victor of the Battle of Gettysburg.

Daniel Sullivan, from Cork, settled in Nansemond County, Virginia, and was subsequently elected to the House of Burgesses. His descendants, who spelled the name Sullivant, were pioneers in the settlement of Ohio.

1691 Daniel MacCarthy, from Cork, settled in Virginia, becoming a Burgess in 1705 and Speaker of the House (1715-20). His son Denis married (1724) Sarah Ball, a first cousin of Mary Ball, George Washington's mother. Washington was a neighbor and intimate friend of his MacCarthy cousins.

1692 William O'Brien, from County Clare, settled in North Carolina. He was the first American ancestor of William Jennings Bryan.

1696 Irish immigrants from Waterford settled in Burlington County, New Jersey.

1699 James Logan (1674-1751), from Armagh, came over as Secretary to William Penn. He subsequently became a member of the provincial council, Mayor of Philadelphia, acting governor (1736-8) and Chief Justice of Pennsylvania. While mayor, he authorized his fellow-Irishmen to attend the first public Mass in Philadelphia.

1703 Daniel Dulany (1685-1753) born in Queen's County, Ireland, arrived in Maryland as an indentured servant. After gaining his freedom he won admission to the Maryland Bar(1710). He became a judge, Attorney General of the province, a member of the legislature (1722-42) and of the Governor's Council (1742-53) and championed the colonial cause in his pamphlet "The Rights of the Inhabitants of Maryland to the Benefit of English laws" (1728). His son, Daniel (1722-97) was secretary of the province of Maryland (1761-74), and leading opponent of the Stamp Act.

1704 Laws discouraging the entry of Catholics into Maryland were passed by the legislature this year and again in 1715. They excluded or imposed duties upon the importation of all "Irish servants." A similar law had been passed in South Carolina in 1698.

1706 Reverend Francis Makemie (1658-1708), from Donegal, organized the first American Presbytery, in Virginia. He had been a "wandering evangelist" since his arrival from Ireland in 1683 and is regarded as the founder of Presbyterianism in America.

1710 Settlers from the north of Ireland, including McDowell, McDuffie, and McGruder families, settled in Blue Ridge region of Virginia.

1718 Earliest organized band of emigrants to leave Ireland in the 18th Century sailed from Donegal. It included about 100 families who settled in New Hampshire at the town of Londonderry.

1720 Noting that some 2,600 Irishmen had arrived in Boston during the past three years, the governor of Massachusetts complained of the "public burden" imposed by the coming of "so many poor people from abroad, especially those that come from Ireland." The General Court of Massachusetts warned immigrants from Ireland to leave the colony within seven months.

1721 Between this date and 1742, over 3,000 immigrants came to America from the province of Ulster alone.

1722 Members of the Presbyterian congregation at Voluntown (near Hartford), Connecticut, petitioned for the removal of their minister, Reverend Samuel Dorrance: "He came out of Ireland, and since his coming, the Irish do flock into town."

Matthew Watson, a native of Ireland, settled at Barrington, Rhode Island and engaged in brick making. He supplied much of the brick for New York's urban expansion during the 18th Century and he remained active in business until over 100 years of age.

1729 Charles Clinton (b. 1690 at Corbay, County Longford) landed at Cape Cod. He and his wife, also a native of Ireland, later settled in New York. Their son James (1733-1812) became a Brigadier General during the Revolutionary War and his son, DeWitt (1769-1828) served as Governor of New York, 1817-21 and 1825-8. George, James' younger brother (1739-1812) held the Governorship 1777-1795 and 1801-04, and served as Vice-President of the United States, 1805-12.

1736 James Patton (born Londonderry, 1692) received a grant of land west of the Blue Ridge Mountains. Augusta County, Virginia was settled largely through his efforts. He crossed the Atlantic 25 times bringing Irish redemptioners. Patton was killed by Indians in 1755.

A band of settlers from Bainbridge, County Down, established themselves on the banks of the Opequan River in the Shenandoah Valley of Virginia.

1737 The Charitable Irish Society was founded on St. Patrick's Day in Boston by 26 Irish immigrants "to aid unfortunate fellow countrymen, to cultivate a spirit of unity and harmony among all Irishmen in the Massachusetts colony and their descendants and to advance their interests socially and morally." This is the oldest Irish society in the United States.

Jeremiah Smith, born in Ireland (1705), came to America (1726) and began operation of the first paper factory in this country, at Dorchester, Massachusetts.

1738 William Johnson (1715-74), a native of Meath (whose original family name was MacShane) settled in the Mohawk Valley, New York. In 1755 he was created a baronet and named Superintendent of Indian Affairs. On his death he was succeeded by his nephew Guy Johnson (1740-88), also born in Ireland, who directed Iroquois attacks against the colonists during the Revolutionary War.

1740 At about this date, Edward and William Patterson, natives of Dungannon, County Tyrone, began the first manufacture of tinware in America, at Berlin and New Britain, Connecticut.

1743 Travelers' accounts refer to "the Irish Tract," a district in the lower Shenandoah Valley occupied by Irish settlements.

1752 Hugh Gaine (1726-1807), a native of Belfast, who came to America in 1745, founded the New York Mercury, which became one of the leading colonial newspapers.

1760 John Lynch, from Galway, settled in Virginia where his elder son, John, founded the town of Lynchburg. His younger son, Colonel Charles Lynch, was a commander of irregular forces during the Revolution and, by his drastic treatment of loyalists, gave rise to the term "Lynch Law." The latter's son, Charles, became Governor of Louisiana.

1762 First recorded celebration of St. Patrick's Day in New York City "in the house of John Marshall at Mount Pleasant, near the College" (i.e., King's College, later Columbia).

1764 Thomas Burke (1747-83) and his brother Adamus (1743-1802) arrived in America. Thomas represented North Carolina in the Continental Congress from 1776-1781, when he was elected Governor of North Carolina; captured by the British, he died shortly thereafter. Adamus Burke was Chief Justice of the South Carolina Supreme Court in 1778 and represented his state in the First Congress, 1789-91.

1765 Matthew Lyon (1750-1811), a native of Wicklow, arrived in America. Settling in Vermont, he aided Ethan Allen in the capture of Fort Ticonderoga (1775) and represented that state in Congress, 1797-1801. After moving south he was elected Congressman from Kentucky, 1803-11.

1768 A band of Irish Methodists, led by Philip Embury (1728-1773), a native of Ballingane, founded the Wesley Chapel on John Street in New York City, the first Methodist church in America.

The Friendly Brothers of St. Patrick, a fraternal organization largely composed of Irish-born officers serving in the British forces in North America, began its existence which extended to the end of the Revolutionary War. Its annual meetings were usually held on St. Patrick's Day in New York City.

1770 Patrick Carr, a native of Ireland, killed in the "Boston Massacre" (March 5).

1771 The Friendly Brothers of St. Patrick founded in Charleston, South Carolina by a group of Irish Americans including John and Edward Rutledge, both of whom subsequently became Governors of South Carolina.

The Pennsylvania Packet commenced publication. At first a weekly, in 1784 it became the first daily newspaper published in the United States. Its owner, John Dunlap (1747-1812) came to America from County Tyrone in 1757, and in 1776, as Printer to the Continental Congress, printed the first copies of the Declaration of Independence.

1772 A decline in the linen trade and exhorbitant rents spurred a new wave of emigration from the north of Ireland. Some 30,000 Ulstermen sailed for America in the five years preceding the Revolutionary War.

1774 A British contingent under Colonel Andrew Lewis (1720-81), a native of Ireland, defeated the Shawnee Indians at Point Pleasant on the Ohio River, opening the way for American penetration of the Northwest Territory during the Revolutionary War. Lewis, who had come to America in 1732 and settled in Virginia, joined the patriots in 1776 and was named a Brigadier General in the Continental Army.

John Sullivan (1740-95), whose father had emigrated from Limerick in 1723, led a band of New Hampshire militia men in the seizure of Fort William and Mary, Newcastle, New Hampshire. The gunpowder captured here was later used at Bunker Hill. Sullivan, hailed as "the first to take up arms against the King" was commissioned a Major General in the Continental Army and in 1779 broke the power of the Iroquois and Loyalists in New York State. He served as Governor of New Hampshire from 1786-1789.

1775 Daniel Boone, accompanied by other pioneers of Irish origin, including McGrady, Harland and McBride, commenced the settlement of Kentucky.

Jeremiah O'Brien (1740-1818), whose father was a native of Cork, captured the British schooner Margaretta in Machias Bay, Maine, on June 12. This first naval action of the Revolution has been called "the Lexington of the Seas." Jeremiah and his brother John commanded American privateers during the War.

General Richard Montgomery (1736-75), a native of Dublin who had come to America in 1772, led a contingent of Continental troops in an invasion of Canada. He captured Montreal, but was killed leading an assault on Quebec City (Dec. 31).

1776 Samuel Loudon (1727-1813), a native of Ireland, founded The New York Packet and American Advertiser, a weekly newspaper.

British troops evacuated Boston on March 17 and General Washington prescribed "St. Patrick" as the password of his army for that day. Among his staff officers during the war were Colonel Stephen Moylan, a native of Cork; Colonel John Fitzgerald, born in Wicklow; and Colonel Francis Barber, whose father, Patrick, had emigrated from Longford.

Declaration of Independence signed in Philadelphia (July). Irish-born signers were Matthew Thornton (1714-1803) of New Hampshire, George Taylor (1716-81) of Pennsylvania and James Smith (1719-1806) of Pennsylvania. Signers of Irish origin included Edward Rutledge, Thomas Lynch, Thomas McKean, George Read, and Charles Carroll. The Secretary of the Congress from 1774 was Charles Thomson (1729-1824) who came to America as an indentured servant after being orphaned at the age of ten. By 1760 he was a prosperous merchant in Philadelphia. It was his duty to read the Declaration before the Congress for the first time (and to notify George Washington of his election to the Presidency in 1789).

1777 Battle of Saratoga (October 7). Sharp-shooter Timothy Murphy of Morgan's Rifle Corps picked off two British Commanders - a major factor in the American victory. Murphy (1750-1818), son of Irish immigrant parents, was the most famous marksman of the Revolution. His exploits ranged over the whole span of the war years and most of its major campaigns.

Hercules Mulligan, an Irish-born tailor in New York City, was appointed Washington's chief "confidential agent." While posing as a collaborator during the British occupation of the city he provided the American commander with vital information on the enemy's plans and movements.

1778 General Sir Henry Clinton, reporting on the American rebels to the Colonial Secretary in London, declared that "The emigrants from Ireland are in general to be looked upon as our most serious antagonists." Men of Irish birth or descent were calculated to have formed between one-third and one-half of the Revolutionary forces, including 1,492 officers and 26 generals (15 of whom were born in Ireland).

1779 The first St. Patrick's Day Parade in New York City took place. It was sponsored by the Volunteers of Ireland, a Loyalist regiment commanded by an Irish peer, Lord Rawdon.

1782 Great Britain recognized Ireland's legislative autonomy and her right to regulate domestic affairs through her own Parliament. The so-called "Revolution" of 1782, which brought this about, was facilitated by Britain's preoccupation with the American War. Exchange of congratulations and felicitations between United States Congress and Irish Parliament in recognition of their common interests and grievances followed this move by Great Britain.

1784 James Duane (1733-97) elected first post-colonial Mayor of New York City. Formerly a member of the Continental Congress (1774-84), he held office until 1789. His father, Anthony Duane, had emigrated from Ireland in 1717.

Friendly Sons of St. Patrick organized as a fraternal and charitable body in New York City. Daniel McCormick, a native of Ireland and a Director of the Bank of New York, elected first president.

Mathew Carey (1760-1839), a leading Dublin newspaper editor, fled to America to escape prosecution for criticism of the British government. He founded the Pennsylvania Herald in 1785 and the Columbian Magazine in 1786 and became a prominent publisher and book seller in Philadelphia. His son, Henry Charles Carey (1793-1879), won renown as an economist.

1785 Dominick Lynch (1754-1825) arrived in New York from his native Galway and soon established himself as one of the leading merchants of the city. His son, Dominick II (d. 1844), was a leader of New York society and a patron of the arts.

1789 General Henry Knox (1750-1806), son of Andrew Knox, an Irish immigrant, appointed Secretary of War in Washington's Cabinet. He had served as Chief of Artillery throughout the Revolutionary War, succeeded Washington as Commander-in-Chief from 1783-1784 and acted as Secretary of War under the Articles of Confederation from 1785 to 1789. He was a member of the Charitable Irish Society of Boston and of the Friendly Sons of St. Patrick in Philadelphia.

1790 The Hibernian Society of Philadelphia founded. Thomas McKean (1734-1817), the son of Irish immigrants and a signer of the Declaration of Independence, was elected first president.

First census of the United States recorded 44,000 Irish-born residents, more than half of them living south of Pennsylvania. Some historians regard this figure as far too low, estimating two or three times as many Irish-born Americans at this date.

1791 James Hoban (1758-1831), a native of Kilkenny who had settled in Charleston after the Revolutionary War and acquired a reputation as an architect, produced the design for a "President's Palace" in the new Federal City (Washington, D. C.). The "Palace," subsequently known as the White House, was modeled upon Leinster House in Dublin.

1793 Society for the Relief of Emigrants from Ireland founded at Philadelphia by Mathew Carey and other leading members of the Irish-American community.

1795 William Duane (1760-1835), a graduate of Trinity College, Dublin, began editorship of The Aurora in Philadelphia. This newspaper was a leading mouthpiece of Thomas Jefferson's Democratic Party. Duane was named adjutant-general during the War of 1812. His son, William John Duane (1780-1865), was Secretary of the Treasury in President Jackson's Cabinet.

1798 Revolutionary uprising of the Society of United Irishmen against British rule in Ireland occurred. After the destruction of their movement many rebels took refuge in the United States. Among these were: Patrick Rogers, whose four sons were eminent scientists, notably William Barton Rogers (1804-82) who became first president of M. I. T.; Robert Adrian, who became Professor of Mathematics and Natural Philosophy at Columbia College; and John Daly Burk, author of a four volume History of Virginia and a political protegé of Jefferson. James McKinley, grandfather of President William McKinley, also emigrated from Antrim at about this time. His brother Francis had been hanged as a United Irish rebel.

1801 Act of Union between Great Britain and Ireland abolished Irish legislative autonomy and created the United Kingdom of Great Britain and Ireland. Repeal of this Act became a major goal of Irish and Irish-American political aspirations.

1803 Benevolent Hibernian Society of Baltimore organized. Its first president was Dr. John Campbell White, a United Irishman who fled Belfast in 1798.

1804 Thomas Addis Emmet (1764-1827), a leader of the United Irishmen, arrived in America after having been banished from Ireland. He was admitted to the New York Bar by a special act of the legislature and in 1812 became attorney general of New York.

1805 William J. Macneven (1763-1841) settled in New York City. Like T. A. Emmet, he was a member of the United Irish Directory and exiled after the 1798 rebellion. He became Professor of Obstetrics at the College of Physicians and Surgeons and "made many distinguished contributions to the advancement of medicine." He was president of the Irish Emigrant Society until his death and elder statesman of the Irish American community. Among his works was . . . Advice to Irishmen Arriving in America, which contained an appendix on the naturalization laws, by T. A. Emmet.

1806 Harman Blennerhasset (1765-1831), whose republican sympathies had led him to emigrate from Kerry, was involved

1806 in Aaron Burr's conspiracy. His estate on Blennerhasset's Island in the Ohio River was the assembly point for Burr's "army" which, according to various versions, was intended for the invasion of Mexico, or the overthrow of the United States Government. Blennerhasset was arrested with Burr but subsequently released without being brought to trial.

1807 James Sullivan (1744-1808) elected Governor of Massachusetts. He was a son of John Sullivan who had come over from Limerick in 1723 and a brother of Major General Sullivan, the conqueror of the Iroquois.

1808 Joseph Carless, a native of Westmeath who had settled in St. Louis after the failure of the 1798 Rebellion, established the Missouri Gazette, the first newspaper west of the Mississippi River.

1810 The Shamrock, first Irish-American newspaper, was published in New York City. It was edited by Thomas O'Connor (1770-1855), a United Irish refugee who became a leader of Tammany Hall, a City Commissioner and (1842) candidate for Mayor of New York.

1811 The American Review of History and Politics, the first quarterly journal in the United States, was started by Robert Walsh (1784-1859), son of an Irish immigrant. Walsh also edited the American Register (1817-18), the National Gazette (1819-36) and the Magazine of Foreign Literature. He served as American Consul at Paris, 1845-51.

1812-15 During the war between the United States and Britain a number of officers of Irish parentage played notable roles: Andrew Jackson, the victor of New Orleans, and later the President of the United States was the son of County Antrim emigrants; the mother of Commodore Oliver H. Perry, victor of Lake Erie, was born in Newry, County Down; Commodore Thomas Macdonough, who defeated the British at Plattsburgh was the grandson of John Macdonough, who came over from Kildare in 1730. In addition, Commodore John Shaw (1773-1823) who emigrated from Ireland in 1790, commanded the United States Naval Squadron in the Mediterranean during the war.

1814 Irish Emigrant society founded in New York City by Dr. Robert Hogan, President of the Friendly Sons of St. Patrick. Its purpose was to meet new arrivals from Ireland, protect them from being exploited by swindlers and boarding-house keepers and aid them in establishing themselves in America.

1815-35 A great era of road and canal building began in the United States; carried out largely by Irish labor drawn from the rising flow of immigrants.

1816 Irish Emigrant Society opened an office in Nassau Street, New York City. Dr. William Macneven organized this service to procure employment for the new wave of Irish refugees which followed the end of the wars in Europe and America.

Archibald Mellon came from County Tyrone and settled in Pennsylvania. His son Andrew married Rebecca Wauchop, also born in Ireland. Their grandson was Andrew Mellon (1855-1937), Secretary of the Treasury, 1921-32 and Ambassador to Britain, whose family remains prominent in industry, finance, and art partonage.

1817 The Irish Emigrant Society petitioned Congress to set aside public lands in Illinois to which new arrivals might go rather than remain in the crowded and corrupting cities of the Eastern seaboard. Congress was asked to "sell land, on fourteen years' credit, to deserving Irishmen, who would serve as a frontier guard against marauding Indians." The petition was rejected by an 83 to 71 vote in the House of Representatives.

1818 Erin Benevolent Society was founded in St. Louis. St. Patrick's Day first celebrated there by Irish immigrants on March 17, 1820.

1820-30 During this decade some 50,000 Irish immigrants entered the United States.

1823-9 The campaign for Catholic Emancipation in Ireland, led by Daniel O'Connell, won sympathy and support of the Irish in America.

1823 James Shields (1810-79), a native of Tyrone, settled in Illinois. He served as a brigadier-general in the Mexican War and held the same rank during the Civil War. In addition to serving as Governor of the Oregon Territory in 1848, he was United States Senator from Illinois, 1849-55, from Minnesota, 1858-9, and from Missouri in 1879---the only man ever to have represented three different states in the United States Senate.

Alexander T. Stewart (1803-76) a native of Lisburn, County Antrim, arrived in the United States in 1820 and opened a small drygoods shop in New York City which developed into the great retail store, A. T. Stewart and Company.

1824 — The National Gazette listed seven Irish-Americans currently serving in the House of Representatives: Jeremiah O'Brien of Maine, George Cassaday of New Jersey, Sameul McKean of Pennsylvania, Louis McLane of Delaware, Henry Connor of North Carolina, Henry Conway of Arkansas and Patrick Farrelly of Pennsylvania (who was born in Ireland). McKean and McLane later became United States Senators and the latter was Secretary of State under President Jackson.

1824 — John McLoughlin (1784-1857), whose father was born in Donegal, became chief Factor for the Hudson's Bay Company at the fur trading post of Fort George near the mouth of the Columbia River. In this capacity he ruled (until 1846) an area now occupied by Oregon, Washington, Northern California, Idaho, and adjacent portions of Nevada and Wyoming, as well as north western Canada as far as the Yukon.

1828 — Two colonies of Irish immigrants were established in Texas, then a province of Mexico. James Power and James Hewitson brought 200 families to Refugio and another 200 families settled at San Patricio under the leadership of John Mullen and Patrick McGloin.

The Friends of Ireland, an association supporting Daniel O'Connell's campaign for Irish Catholic Emancipation, was formed in New York under the presidency of Dr. William Macneven. Branches were established throughout the United States and in Mexico, and large sums of money were collected and forwarded to Ireland to aid the cause.

1830-40 — During this decade 540,000 immigrants, of whom 44% were Irish, entered the United States. At this time the United States had a population of only 13 million.

1833 — At this date there were an estimated 40,000 Irish-born residents of New York City.

1834 — An anti-Catholic riot occurred in Charlestown, Massachusetts where an Ursuline Convent was burned. Growing anti-Catholic and anti-foreign feeling in United States was stimulated by increased Irish immigration and competition in the job market.

Charles O'Malley, a native of Mayo and fur trader on Mackinac Island, promoted a large-scale immigration of settlers from his native county into Michigan.

1835 — Thomas Jefferson Rusk (1803-57), son of an Irish immigrant stonemason, who settled in Texas, was a member of the convention that proclaimed Texas an independent republic. He served successively as Secretary of War, Commander-in-Chief of the army and Chief Justice of the Supreme

Court. In 1845 he was president of the convention which voted for annexation to the United States, and along with Sam Houston (also descended from Irish immigrants) he was one of this state's first United States Senators.

1837 Edmund O'Callaghan (1797-1880), a native of Mallow, County Cork, settled in Albany and devoted himself to historical research. Among his writings: A History of New Netherlands (1846), A Documentary History of New York (1849-51), Documents Relative to the Colonial History of New York (1855-61).

The Bond Street Riot took place in Boston. Continued friction between Irish immigrants and "Yankees" who feared the growing numbers of the newcomers was the cause of the trouble.

1840-50 During this decade nearly 800,000 Irish immigrants entered the United States.

1841-6 A campaign, led by Daniel O'Connell, waged for Repeal of the Act of Union between Britain and Ireland. O'Connell's insistence on non-violence and his willingness to maintain an Anglo-Irish connection under the Crown, alienated many Irish-Americans and led to a divided attitude towards the Repeal movement in America.

1843 Anti-Irish nativism inspired formation of an "American Republican Party" pledged to securing a 21 year-residence requirement for naturalization.

1844 Anti-Catholic riots erupted in Philadelphia. Irish neighborhoods were invaded by nativist mobs: 30 killed, 150 wounded, 200 families burned out, 3 churches destroyed.

1845-7 The Phrase "Manifest Destiny," as an embodiment of the American concept of expansion, was coined by John L. O'Sullivan, editor of the Democratic Review, 1836-45. O'Sullivan, son of an immigrant, was one of the first Irish-Americans to receive a diplomatic appointment, serving as Minister to Portugal, 1854-8.

A potato blight in Ireland destroyed the basic food crop of the Irish masses. Thousands perished; hundreds of thousands, fleeing famine and disease, emigrated to America.

1847 United States went to war with Mexico. In addition to an uncounted number of Irish-American soldiers in the invading army, there were some 2,000 recent immigrants from Ireland serving under Generals Scott and Taylor. Notable among the officers of Irish origin were General William O. Butler, who succeeded Scott as commander-in-chief in

Mexico (Feb. 1848) and General S. W. Kearny, who directed the conquest of California.

1848 — An armed insurrection broke out in Ireland. It was led by the Young Ireland movement, whose leaders had broken with O'Connell's Repeal Association over the issues of violent revolution and separatist nationalism. After the failure of the rebellion, Young Ireland chieftans such as John Mitchel, Thomas D'Arcy McGee, and Thomas F. Meagher found refuge in the United States and played a leading part in Irish-American journalism and politics.

Hibernian Benevolent Society established in Chicago.

1850-60 — During this decade over 900,000 Irish immigrants entered the United States.

1851 — Emigrant Industrial Savings Bank chartered in New York under sponsorship of the Irish Emigrant Society.

1855 — Irish immigrants of the first generation comprised 34% of all voters in New York City. Over 300 of the city's 1,100 policemen at this date were Irish-born.

1857 — William Kelly (1811-88) patented a converter for the making of steel. He was the son of an Irish immigrant who arrived in Pittsburgh in 1801.

1858 — The Fenian Brotherhood (more formally known as the Irish Republican Brotherhood) founded in New York. An oath-bound secret revolutionary organization, it was committed to the use of violence to attain Irish independence. Its principal organizer was John O'Mahoney (1816-77) who had fled Ireland after the failure of the 1848 rebellion.

1859 — William W. Corcoran (1798-1888), son of an Irish immigrant, founded the Corcoran Gallery of Art in Washington, D. C.. He had made a fortune in mercantile and financial transactions.

1860 — New York became the "largest Irish city in the world," with an Irish-born population of 203,740 out of a total population of 805,651. The neighboring, but then independent, city of Brooklyn had 56,710 natives of Ireland out of 266,661 residents.

1861-5 — In the War Between the States (Civil War), nearly 150,000 natives of Ireland served in the Union forces, with exclusively Irish regiments formed in New York, Massachusetts, Michigan, Ohio, Indiana, Illinois and Iowa. Among the notable officers of Irish origin were Generals Philip H. Sheridan, T. W. Sweeney, St. Clair Mulholland, Philip Kearny, Michael Corcoran, and Thomas F. Meagher, an exiled leader of the 1848 rebellion who raised the famed "Irish Brigade."

The estimated 85,000 Irish-born residents of the Confederate States of America and those of Irish descent residing in the South rallied overwhelmingly to the cause of States' Rights. Stephen Mallory of Florida and James Reagan of Texas served in President Davis' Cabinet, while Generals Patrick Cleburne, Joseph Finegan and John Adams led regiments in the field that included the Emerald Guards of Alabama, the Emerald Light Infantry of South Carolina and the Emmet Guards of Virginia.

1865 William Russell Grace (1832-1904), a native of Queenstown, County Cork, founded W. R. Grace and Company to engage in trade with South America. He later organized the New York and Pacific Steamship Company and the Grace Steamship Company and was elected Mayor of New York in 1880 and 1884.

1866 An invasion of Canada by Fenian forces ("Irish Republican Army") was led by John O'Neill (1834-78), a native of Monaghan and former United States Army officer. His troops, veterans of the Union army, defeated British detachments on June 2 but were obliged to withdraw after United States Government intervention.

1867 The Fenian revolt failed in Ireland. Clan na-Gael was founded as a secret, oath-bound society dedicated to promoting republicanism in Ireland, organizing Irish-Americans to help Ireland and opposing British influence in the U. S. It absorbed some members of the Fenian Brotherhood who were dissatisfied with that organization's internal squabblings and leadership rivalries.

1870 Patrick Ford (1835-1913), a native of Galway, founded The Irish World in New York City. It is the oldest of the major Irish-American newspapers still being published.

1871 John Devoy, Jeremiah O'Donovan Rossa and other Fenian leaders banished from Ireland arrived in New York City and were welcomed with a parade and civic reception. They gave their endorsement to the Clan na-Gael, rather than to any of the other competing factions of the Fenian Brotherhood.

1872 Charles O'Conor(1804-1884), nationally-famed New York attorney and prosecutor of the Tweed Ring, was nominated for the Presidency of the United States by the "Straight-Out Democrats" who refused to accept Horace Greeley, the regular Democratic candidate. Son of the 1798 exile Thomas O'Connor, he was the first Catholic ever nominated, though he declined to run.

1873 Augustus Saint Gaudens (1848-1907), born in Dublin of a French father and an Irish mother, set up his studio in New York City and began a career which brought him world-renown as a sculptor.

John William Mackay (1831-1902), a native of Dublin who arrived in the U. S. in 1840, struck gold in Nevada. He built a fortune in mining and supported the project of a Transatlantic Cable in the 1880's.

1876 "Last Stand" of the (predominantly Irish) 7th Cavalry under Gen. Custer dramatized in the public imagination the role played by Irish-American soldiers and frontiersmen in the "Winning of the West."

1878 Michael Davitt, "Father of the Land League," toured the U. S. and conferred with Irish-American leaders, advocating an attack on the landholding system in Ireland.

1879 The Irish National Land League was founded in Dublin. "Land War" began in Ireland (to 1882), marked by tenant resistance to landlords, boycotting, etc.

Terence V. Powderly (1849-1924) elected Grand Master Workman (to 1893) of the Knights of Labor, the first national labor union (founded 1869). Its 800,000 members included thousands of Irish-Americans. Powderly, the son of Irish immigrants, was instrumental in obtaining legislation favorable to labor in many states and in collaboration with James Cardinal Gibbons (1834-1921), Archbishop of Baltimore, brought about a more liberal attitude in the American Catholic Church on labor questions.

The "Molly Maguire" movement, a revival of an earlier terrorist organization of the same name in the Pennsylvania coal-mining districts, came to an end with the execution of its leaders, who were Irish-Americans. The police agent and the prosecutor who brought them to justice were also Irish-Americans.

1880 Charles Stewart Parnell, President of the Land League and leader of the Irish Home Rule movement, toured the U. S. to raise funds and to win Irish-American support for agrarian reform in Ireland. He addressed Congress on February 2.

Irish National Land League of the United States founded (May), with hundreds of branches established by mid-summer.

New York Society for the Preservation of the Irish Language sponsored concerts of Gaelic songs and encouraged study of ancient Irish language as a stimulus to pride in national origin. Beginning of widespread literary and cultural programs in Irish-American community.

1881 National Land League Convention in Chicago was attended by 850 delegates; a quarter of a million dollars was subscribed to aid "Land War."

John Philip Holland (1840-1914), a native of County Clare who had arrived in the U. S. in 1873 and pursued research in submarine navigation, launched his first successful submarine, the Fenian Ram. The project had been sponsored by the Fenian Brotherhood, which sought a means of destroying the British fleet, but defects in the power system rendered her useless for extended voyages. The inventor continued his experiments and in 1898 launched the Holland at Elizabeth, N. J. This submarine was purchased by the U. S. Government in 1900 and became the prototype of a new category of warship.

1882-3 Divisions increased among Irish-Americans over the situation in Ireland. Clan na-Gael, dominated by John Devoy, advocated more radical measures than those approved by the Land Leaguers, led by John Boyle O'Reilly, editor of the Boston Pilot, and Patrick Collins (a future mayor of Boston).

1884 The Ancient Order of Hibernians made all Roman Catholics of Irish descent eligible for membership. Founded in 1836 as a secret society limited to native-born Irishmen, it acquired a sinister notoriety in connection with labor violence in Pennsylvania. Henceforth its program would include "agitation for Irish freedom, ardent support of the Church and the stimulation of interest in Irish history, culture and folklore."

Samuel S. McClure (1857-1949), a native of Antrim, established the McClure Syndicate, the first newspaper syndicate in the U. S. He was also the founder and editor of McClure's Magazine (1893).

1885 The last convention of the Fenian Brotherhood in America was held. The Society could no longer command active, extensive support among Americans.

Hugh O'Brien, a native of Fermanagh, was elected Mayor of Boston, thus marking the rise of Irish-American political activity in that city.

1886 Victor Herbert (1859-1924), a native of Dublin, arrived in the U. S. to begin his career as the major American composer of light opera.

1888 Irish-American political pressure forced President Cleveland to expel the British Ambassador, Sir Lionel Sackville-West, after the latter had expressed confidence that British interests would be safe while Cleveland was in office.

1890 Michael Cudahy (1841-1910), a native of Kilkenny, founded the Cudahy Packing Co., one of the principal meat-packing corporations in the U. S.

Alfred Thayer Mahan (1840-1914) published The Influence of Seapower Upon History, the most famous of his numerous historical volumes and strategical studies. Admiral Mahan, as President of the Naval War College (1886-9, 1892-3) and author, exercised a decisive influence upon American and European geopolitical thinking. He and his father, Dennis Hart Mahan (1802-71), professor of Engineering at West Point, 1832-71, were descendants of an eighteenth-century Irish immigrant.

1891 The Irish National Federation of America was organized in New York City under the presidency of Dr. T. A. Emmet, grandson of the 1798 leader. About 150 chapters were established and funds were raised to aid the cause of home rule in Ireland. This "unworthy compromise" was rejected by those who demanded an independent republic.

1893 Foundation of the Gaelic League in Ireland was promptly followed by the establishment of branches in the U. S. and a series of annual national conventions. The League sought to promote the study of the Irish language and the revival of a distinct national culture. Newspapers in Ireland welcomed a "Gaelic Revival in America."

Louis H. Sullivan (1856-1924), son of a County Cork emigrant, designed the Transportation Building for the World's Columbian Exposition, one of the major steps in a career that earned him the title of "father of modernism in architecture."

The "Mr. Dooley" sketches by Finley Peter Dunne (1867-1936), Irish-American essayist, first appeared (October 10).

1895 — The Irish National Alliance was established in the U. S. to campaign against any Anglo-American "entanglements."

1897 — The American Irish Historical Society was founded "to make better known the Irish chapter in American history."

Joseph McKenna (1843-1926) appointed Attorney General of the United States, the first Irish-American Catholic to hold Cabinet office. He served as an Associate Justice of the Supreme Court from 1898 to 1925.

1898-9 — Widespread opposition existed among Irish-Americans to the new U. S. policy of "imperialistic" expansion after the Spanish-American War. William Jennings Bryan addressed mass demonstration by 15,000 members of the United Irish Societies in Chicago, condemning "imperialism, militarism, and the trusts," and won Irish-American support during the 1900 presidential campaign.

1900 — President McKinley was accused of importing "imperialism, a plant of English growth," and of promoting a secret alliance with Britain to advance colonialism. The Irish World asked: "Shall Porto Rico become America's Ireland?"

A convention was held at Atlantic City, N. J. to unite the various groups claiming to perpetuate the Fenian tradition. The Clan na-Gael emerged as the dominant force in the Irish nationalist movement in America.

Thomas Fortune Ryan (1851-1928) gained control of the New York City transportation lines. The financial empire of this Virginia-born descendant of Irish immigrants also included holdings in tobacco, banking, insurance, railroads and rubber and mining interests in Africa and America.

1903 — The Gaelic American was established in New York City by John Devoy as the organ of the Clan na-Gael.

Henry Ford (1863-1947) established the Ford Motor Co., the world's largest manufacturer of automobiles. He was the grandson of John Ford, who emigrated from County Cork in 1847 and settled in Michigan.

1904 In an effort to coordinate American support for Irish independence, the United Irish League held a convention in New York City attended by delegates from 33 states and by representatives from Ireland.

1905-7 Dr. Douglas Hyde (1860-1945), President of the Gaelic League--and later first President of Ireland--lectured in the United States and received large donations from Irish-Americans to carry on the work of the League.

1907 The Ancient Order of Hibernians and National German-American Alliance agreed "to combine forces againt foreign entanglements, further restrictions on immigration, and inroads on personal liberty."

Maurice F. Egan (1852-1924), an Irish-American writer and educator was appointed Minister to Denmark; he negotiated (1916) purchase by U. S. of Danish West Indies (now Virgin Islands).

1911-12 There was bitter Irish-American opposition to the Anglo-American Arbitration Treaty; it was approved by President Taft but rejected by the Senate after outcry against "entangling alliances."

1914 A monument to John Barry was unveiled by President Wilson. He spoke of Barry as "an Irishman whose heart crossed the Atlantic with him, unlike some Americans, who needed hyphens in their names, because only part of them has come over. Protests by Irish-American groups over this "defamation of their loyalty" sparked the beginning of the "hyphenated Americans" controversy, which lasted throughout Wilson's presidency.

The European War began (August). Strong anti-British sentiment among Irish-Americans. German propagandists were active in Irish-American circles.

1915 A joint rally of Irish- and German-Americans took place at Madison Square Garden, New York City, culminating in the formation of the "Friends of Peace," dedicated to keeping America from entering the War on England's side.

1916 A convention of the "Irish Race in America" was held at the Hotel Astor in New York City. The 2,300 delegates gathered "to reassert Ireland's claim to nationhood and to demand that the United States keep out of the War." (March).

An uprising in Dublin and the proclamation of an Irish Republic (April) known as the "Easter Rebellion" was soon crushed by Britain. Outrage among Irish-Americans over the swift and brutal execution of the nationalist leaders led to the beginning of more serious and sympathetic attention to the Irish Question in U. S. press and public opinion.

1917 Entry of the United States into the War was given wholehearted support by a majority of the Irish-American community, despite earlier agitation for neutrality. Distinguished military service was contributed by Irish-American commanders such as Generals John O'Ryan and Thomas Barry and units such as the "Fighting 69th" Regiment.

A cablegram to the British Prime Minister urged settlement of the Irish Question, signed by 134 members of the U. S. House of Representatives.

1918 Continued anti-British agitation by Devoy and his associates was seen as a reflection upon the patriotism of Irish-Americans. The Ancient Order of Hibernians "resented the fact that the conduct of a few extremists could put the loyalty of the Irish race. . . on trial before a tribunal of American public opinion," and called upon the Government to "stamp out treason and sedition which is being openly conducted under the guise of Irish patriotism."

The First World War ended (November). Elections in Ireland resulted in a Republican victory and the beginning of an Anglo-Irish guerrilla war (December). A rally of "Irish Republicans" at Madison Square Garden demanded "justice for Ireland."

1919 At an Irish Race Convention in Philadelphia Irish independence was endorsed and financial support pledged to "patriots" (March).

During the Conference at Versailles, F. P. Walsh, a Kansas city attorney, M. J. Ryan, a Philadelphia banker, and E. P. Dunne, ex-Governor of Illinois, as unofficial spokesmen of the Irish-American community urged President Wilson's intervention on behalf of Ireland. Wilson was embarassed by their presence but no support was forthcoming for Ireland's claim to independence.

Eamon De Valera, President of the Dail Eireann (the Irish Parliament), returned to New York, his native city, and began a U. S. tour to sell Republican bonds, ultimately raising some $5 million.

1920 There was a breach between De Valera and the American Friends of Irish Freedom, which had been sponsoring his tour. Devoy became suspicious of De Valera's political intentions and plans for use of funds. He, in turn, was accused by De Valera's supporters of trying to dictate to Irish-Americans. In November the American Association for the Recognition of the Irish Republic was set up under De Valera's inspiration to by-pass Devoy and his associates.

American Friends of Irish Freedom opposed the League of Nations as "an instrument to increase the influence of the British Empire in international affairs." In the Presidential election, James M. Cox, the Democratic candidate, was abandoned by many Irish-American voters because of his support of the League and because Wilson had failed to include the independence of Ireland in the peace treaty. Cox later attributed his defeat to "the professional Irish."

1921 The Anglo-Irish War was brought to an end by an agreement between moderate Irish leaders and Britain (December 6), creating the Irish Free State with dominion status, and leaving six heavily-Protestant counties of Ulster under British rule as "Northern Ireland."

1922 Civil War in Ireland broke out between the Free State Government and De Valera's Republicans, who refused to accept anything less than a united Irish sovereign state. Attempts by some Clan na-Gael leaders to rouse massive Irish-American opposition to the Free State regime were unsuccessful.

1923 Irish Civil War ended with the surrender of De Valera and his partisans, who ultimately agreed to work within the Free State political system. Most Irish-Americans, satisfied with the virtual independence of Ireland, turned their attention to purely American issues.

1923-8 A feeling of "let down" after the Irish Question faded was paralleled by a sense of neglect, as the Republican Administration in Washington paid little attention to the Irish-American community. Pierce Butler was named to the Supreme Court in 1923, William J. Donovan became Assistant Attorney General and Patrick J. Hurley became Secretary of War in Hoover's Cabinet, but few other Irishmen achieved recognition.

1928 Alfred E. Smith (1873-1944) was nominated for the Presidency of the United States by the Democratic Party. Smith (Governor of New York, 1919-20, 1923-8) was the first Catholic of Irish origin nominated by a major party. He was enthusiastically supported by many Irish-Americans and his defeat, after a campaign that saw the revival of many old religious and social antagonisms, was a fresh source of frustration for them.

1930-40 This was a decade of major achievement for Irish-Americans in the Theater, Films, Literature: Eugene O'Neill won the Nobel Prize in 1936; F. Scott Fitzgerald, John O'Hara, and James T. Farrell won fame as novelists; John Ford twice won the directorial award of the Motion Picture Academy; the Barrymores, and a score of others distinguished themselves on stage and screen.

1933 The advent of Franklin D. Roosevelt and the New Deal brought about a new era of opportunity for Irish-Americans in national politics: Thomas Walsh and later Frank Murphy as Attorney General; James A. Farley as Postmaster General and party manager; Thomas G. Corcoran as presidential adviser; John McCormack as strategist in the House of Representatives, and Joseph P. Kennedy as Ambassador to Great Britain.

1937-40 Renewed antagonism between the Dublin and London Governments and the outbreak of a new European War lead to the revival of activity by nationalist extremists of the Irish Republican Army. There was fear among Irish-Americans that Britain would violate Irish neutrality and occupy the naval and air bases which De Valera had denied her.

1941 A cablegram was sent to Premier De Valera by 129 prominent Irish-Americans asking that Irish air and naval bases be turned over to Britain to aid in the fight against Nazi aggression (March). The signers were denounced by _The Gaelic American:_ "Most of the signers have never taken part in any Irish organizations and their services to Ireland are non-existent." American Friends of Irish Neutrality was formed to oppose Irish involvement in the War.

The Committee for American Irish Defense was formed by Gen. O'Ryan and other Irish-American notables; they published an open letter to President Roosevelt: "You can count on the Irish, Mr. President," and urged the establishment of American air and naval bases in Ireland "to preserve the Freedom of the Seas and to keep inviolate our Icelandic outpost . . ." The Committee sought 100,000 Irish-American signatures to their letter (November). _The Gaelic American_ denounced the Committee as a tool of the Administration and predicted that Irish-American civil servants would be coerced into signing it.

The Japanese attacked Pearl Harbor and America entered into the War against the Axis Powers (December). There was a general rallying of the Irish-American community to the national defense.

1942-5 There was general enthusiasm over Irish-American war heroes such as Captain Colin Kelly, although continued neutrality of the Irish Free State caused some resentment. President Roosevelt warned Britain that any move against Ireland would have unfavorable political repercussions in U. S.

1945-9 Irish-Americans continued to be important in national politics, notably in the Chairmanship of the Democratic National Committee and in the Administration. James Byrnes, the son of Irish-born settlers in South Carolina, was Secretary of State and Maurice Tobin was Secretary of Labor.

1949 The Proclamation of an Irish Republic ended last links with British Commonwealth and confirmed pride of Irish-Americans in the sovereign nationhood of their ancestral homeland. Full U. S. diplomatic relations established with Ireland. The remaining question of Partition ceased to engross the attention of most Irish-Americans, who appeared content to leave it to time and negotiation.

1950-55 There were wide disputes in the Irish-American community over the character and tactics of Senator Joseph McCarthy of Wisconsin.

1960 John Fitzgerald Kennedy elected President of the United States. The great-grandson of Irish immigrants in both ancestral lines, he was the first Irish-American Catholic to hold this office. His election was seen by many as proof that the Irish had "arrived," in the sense of complete acceptance into the American mainstream.

1963 President Kennedy visited Ireland (June). Later in the year (November 22) while in Dallas, Texas, he was killed by an assassin's bullet.

1968 Senator Robert F. Kennedy, brother and political heir of the late President and himself a Presidential candidate, was assassinated.

Civil Rights agitation began among Catholics in Northern Ireland.

1969 Continuing agitation in Northern Ireland lead to Protestant-Catholic rioting (August). Civil Rights leaders from Ulster sought financial and moral support among Irish-Americans.

1970 Violence in Northern Ireland continued and the Irish Republican Army revived its guerrilla campaign to end Partition and unite Ireland. Numerous committees and organizations were formed among Irish-Americans to work on behalf of Civil Rights in Ulster and for Irish unification.

1971 The internment without trial of hundreds of Catholics in Northern Ireland lead to intensified fighting between IRA and British troops (August). There were protests and demonstrations by Irish-Americans and demands that the U. S. Government exert pressure for settlement on Britain.

1972 Thirteen demonstrators were killed by British soldiers in Londonderry (January 30--"Bloody Sunday"). There was outrage in the United States and demands in U. S. Congress for concessions by Britain. The London Government superseded the Northern Ireland administration and offerred redress of grievances, but guerrilla warfare continued. Once again the Irish in America were concerned about their homeland, with responses ranging from sympathy and prayers to the clandestine shipment of weapons.

These turbulent events have led to a marked revival of Irish-American cultural identity.

DOCUMENTS

THE LAND THEY LEFT BEHIND THEM

Sources: (a) Historical Manuscripts Commission, Second Report, London, 1871, p. 257; (b) Proclamation of the Hearts of Steel, March 23, 1772 in the Public Record Office of Northern Ireland, D. 654; (c) Londonderry Journal, April 17, 1832.

IRELAND IN 1716, FROM A LETTER BY JONATHAN SWIFT

The people have already given their bread, their flesh, their butter, their shoes, their stockings, their house furniture and houses to pay their landlords and taxes. I cannot see how any more can be got from them, except we take away their potatoes and buttermilk, or flay them and sell their skins.

IRELAND IN 1772, FROM A PROCLAMATION OF THE "HEARTS OF STEEL," A SECRET SOCIETY FORMED TO RESIST OPPRESSIVE LANDLORDS.

. . . Behold the deplorable state to which oppression has brought us, by reason of heavy rents which are so great a burden to us that we are not scarcely able to bear . . . that one and all . . . are grievious to be born; so that betwixt landlord and rectors, the very marrow is screwed out of our bones, and our lives are even become so burdensome to us, by these uncharitable and unreasonable men, that we do not care whether we live or die; for they lay such burthen upon our shoulders that they cannot touch them with one of their fingers; they have reduced us to such a deplorable state by such grievious oppressions that the poor is turned black in the face, and the skin is parched on their back, that they are rendered incapable to support their starving families with the common necessaries of life, that nature is but scarcely supported, that they have not even food, nor yet raiment to secure them from the extremities of the weather wither by day or night . . . .

IRELAND IN 1832

FROM AN EDITORIAL IN THE LONDONDERRY JOURNAL

Most of those who have sailed from this port this season are, as usual, small farmers who have been in decent circumstances, of the Protestant persuasion. Rackrents . . . combined with tithes, are doubtless the chief cause of the melancholy determination which these persons have adopted; but we can well suppose that there are not a few of them who are anxious to find in the forests of the new world a refuge from the feuds and bickerings which prevail to such a deplorable extent in their own country.

LETTER FROM JAMES MURRAY, AN IMMIGRANT RESIDING IN NEW YORK CITY, TO REV. BAPTIST BOYD, MINISTER OF AUGHELOW, CO. TYRONE, NOVEMBER 7, 1737.

Source: Bradford's New York "Gazette," No. 627, quoted in J. D. Crimmins, Irish American Historical Miscellany, New York, 1905.

Read this letter, and look, and tell aw the poor Folk of your Place, that God has opened a Door for their Deliverance; for here is ne scant of Bread, and if your Sons Samuel and James Boyd wad but come here, they wad get more Money in ane year for teechin a Lettin Skulle, nor ye yer sell wad get for Three Years Preechin whar ye are . . . . The Young Foke in Ereland are but a Pack of Couards, for I will tell ye in short, this is a bonny Country, and aw things grows here that ever I did see grow in Erelad; and wee hea Cows and Sheep and Horses plenty here, and Goats, and Deers, and Raccoons, and Moles, and Bevers, and Fish, and Fouls of aw Sorts. Trades are ow gud nere, a Wabster gets 12 Pence a Year, a Labourer gets 4 Shillings and 5 Pence a Day, a Lass gets 4 Shillings and 6 Pence a Week for spinning . . . a Carpenter gets 6 shillings a Day, and a Tailor gets 20 Shillings for making a Suit of Cleaths . . . Indian Corn, a Man wull get a Bushell of it for his Day's Work here; Rye grows here, and Oats and Wheet, and Winter Barley, and Summer Barley; Buck Wheet grows here, na every Thing grows here . . . .

Now I beg of ye aw to come out here, and bring out wee ye aw the Cleaths ye can of every Sort . . . and Guns, and Pooder, and Shot, and aw Sorts of Weers that is made of Iron and Steel, and Tradesmen that come here let them bring their Tools wee them . . . fetch Whapsaws here, and Hatchets and Augurs and Axes and Spades, and Shov els . . . and aw Sorts of Garden Seeds . . . Potatoes grows here very big . . . ye may clear as muckle Grund to plant Indian Corn in ane Month, as will maintain Ten Folk for a Year . . . .

I ha been 120 Miles in the Wolderness, and there I saw a Plain of Grund 120 Miles lang, and 15 Bred, and where never gree nor Tree upon it, and I hea see as gud Meedow upon it, as ever I see in Ereland . . . . Ye may get Lan here for 10 Pund a Hundred Acres for ever, and Ten Years Tell ye get the Money before they wull ask ye for it; and it is within 40 Miles of this York upon a River Side that this Lan lies, so that ye may carry aw the Guds in Boat to this York to sell, if ony of you comes here . . . .desire my Fether and Mether too, and my Three Sisters to come here, and ye may acquaint them, there are Lads enough here . . . . and I will pay their passage . . . for here aw that a man works for is his ane, there are ne Revenus Hunds to rive it from us here . . . there is ne yen to tak awa yer Corn, yer Potatoes . . . or Eggs . . . .

I bless the Lord for my safe Journey here . . . this York is as big as twa of Armagh . . . . There is servants comes here out of Armagh . . . There is servants comes here out of Ereland, and have served there time here, wha are now Justices of the Piece . . .

LETTER FROM JOHN SMILIE, IRISH IMMIGRANT IN PENNSYLVANIA, TO HIS FATHER, NOVEMBER 11, 1762.

Source: Published in the Belfast News Letter, May 13, 1763, as a warning to other prospective immigrants.

I Account it my Honour and Duty to give you an Account of myself and my Proceedings since I left you; which have, I confess, been a little extraordinary. On the next Tuesday after I left you, I came on Board the S_______y, on the Monday following, being the 24th of May last, we sailed for America: On the 31st we lost Sight of Ireland, having been detained 'till then by Calms and contrary Winds, which seemed to be the doleful Presages of our after unhappy Voyage. We had our full Allowance of Bread and Water only for the first Fortnight; then we were reduced to three Pints of Water per day, and three Pounds and a Half of Bread per Week, to each Person; which it never afterwards exceeded the whole Passage. We had a South-west wind, which drove us so far North, that our Weather became extremely cold, with much Rain and hard Gales of Wind: On the 5th of July we had a hard squal of Wind which lasted 3 Hours, and caused us to lie to; on the 6th we had a Storm which continued 9 Hours, and obliged us to lie to under bare Poles; on the 12th we espied a Mountain of Ice of prodigious Size; on the 13th our weather became more moderate; on the 16th we espied a Sail, which was along Side of us before either saw the other; she having the Wind right aft crowded Sail, and bore away; we gave her Chase, and fired six Guns at her but the Fog soon hid her from us. In this manner did the Captain behave, giving Chase to all Ships he saw, whether they bore off us East or West, it was all alike, the Motives of which caused various Conjectures. August the first our Weather became extremely warm, and the Crew very weak: The 10th Day our Allowance of Bread came to two Pounds and a Half per Week to each Passanger; next week we had only one Pound and a Half; and the next twelve Days we lived upon two Biscuits and a Half for that Time, and half a Noggin of Barley each, make no Use of it, for Thirst; for we were a week that we had but half a Pint of Water per Day for each Person. Hunger and Thirst had now reduced our Crew to the last Extremity; nothing was now to be heard aboard our Ship but the cries of distressed Children, and of their distressed Mothers, unable to relieve them. Our Ship was now truly a real Spectacle of Horror! Never a Day passed without one or two of our Crew put over Board; many kill'd themselves by drinking Salt Water . . . yet in the midst of all our Miseries, our Captain showed not the least remorse or Pity. We were now out of Hopes of ever seeing land. August 29th we had only one Pint of Water for each Person . . . and our Bread was done: But on that Day the Lord was pleased to send the greatest Shower of Rain I ever saw, which was the Means of preserving our Lives . . . . On the first of September we sounded and found ourselves in forty Fathom Water, and the next Morning, about eight o'clock, we saw Land, to the inexpressible Joy of all our Ship's Crew; and on Sunday Morning the 4th of Sept. we came to an anchor off Newcastle; so that we had a passage of fourteen weeks and five Days. You may judge of Captain T______'s Temper and Character by this, that notwithstanding all the Straits we were in for Bread and Water, neither he, nor his Mistress, nor five others that were his Favourites, ever came to Allowance. We had now, since the Time of our setting Sail, lost sixty-four of our Crew by Death. Monday the fifth I came on Shore, and by the Blessing of God, in three Weeks' Time I got perfectly well; but indeed, few of our Ship's Crew were so strong as I; for notwithstanding all I suffered I enjoyed a State of Health the whole Passage. . . .

THE SALE OF INDENTURED SERVANTS, DESCRIBED BY DR. WILLIAMS, AN AMERICAN COLONIST, TO A COMMITTEE OF THE HOUSE OF COMMONS.

Source: Belfast News Letter, March 22, 1774.

. . . It appeared that a trade was carried on in human flesh between Pennsylvania and the province of Ulster. Such of the unhappy natives of that part of Ireland as cannot find employment at home, sell themselves to the masters of vessels, or persons coming from America to deal in that species of merchandise. When they are brought to Philadelphia . . . they are either sold aboard the vessel, or by public vendue, which sale on arrival there is public notice given of, either by handbill, or in the newspapers. They bring generally about fifteen pounds currency at market, are sold for the term of their indentures, which is from two to four years, and on its expiration, receive a suit of clothes, and implements of husbandry, consisting of a hoe, an axe, and a bill from their taskmasters. Several gentlemen in the committee expressed their abhorrence of such a barbarous traffic . . . .

NEWSPAPER EDITORIAL STATEMENT

Source: The Shamrock, Vol, I, No. 1, New York, Dec. 15, 1810.

. . . . Our paper, freed from party bickerings and partial details, shall, on the whole, be a general recorder of noteworthy news, and, particularly as it respects Ireland, a literary and historical panorama of passing events . . . .

It is our wish, and shall be our editorial study, to unite Americans and Irishmen by a bond of friendly intercourse and political amity, having for its object the general good. Gratitude, the first of all moral virtues, will always trace the conduct to be pursued by the Irishman and convince him how conscientiously he should discharge the debt he owes to the nation which, throwing open to him all the advantages of being free in the midst of freedom, offers the greatest encouragement and reward for any employment of art or essay of genius.

As to native Americans, we shall endeavour to impress the political strength and general advantages derivable to them from the residence of a people who, instilled with a love of liberty triumphing even over their constitutional love of country, would separate themselves from their green fields, their health-bestowing climate, and their best friends, to seek an association and residence with a people whom they knew but by character, and in a country of which they knew still less. The characteristic hospitality of the Irishman receives, in his own country, an additional impulse when exercised towards the visiting American. A corresponding sentiment should ever warm the heart of the American at home . . . . from this reciprocation of friendship and good offices, we confidently anticipate the happy result of harmony and cooperation . . . .

On the general subject of national allegiance, it is not our province to descant further than to say that every inhabitant owes allegiance to the government by which he is protected during his residence under the same. If he is a sojourner or an alien, every political interference not warranted or required by the Law is presumptuous and improper; if naturalized, the country of his adoption, by conferring a new favour, acquires a new and indispensable right to every aid that his talent or enterprise, his head, his hand, and his heart can contribute to the protection of his adopted country . . . .

IRISH EMIGRATION TO AMERICA, AS SEEN BY THE SUN OF LONDON

Source: Quoted in The Dublin Evening Post, January 9, 1815.

The minds of the ignorant are acted on by every means which treachery and falsehood can invent; the disaffected part of the Press is zealously at work; every disloyal engine is employed which can delude the mistaken population of the Sister Island into a persuasion that an earthly Paradise exists on the other side of the Atlantic.

We know not what measures Government have taken, or may take, to counteract this conspirarcy. Something, and something effective, must be done; for the mischief is great; and the evil hideous. Were it only the Catholic Agitators . . . and other midnight Assassins who desired to enter into nearer fellowship with kindred spirits elsewhere--with the semi-savages of Kentucky and the scalping Heroes of the United States, we should advise our rulers to provide them with food, clothing, ships, and a premium on exportation; but we should lament for the sake of individuals who might be misled by these tempters, were any considerable number of the People to be deceived into this fatal experiment.

LETTER FROM JOHN DOYLE, IRISH IMMIGRANT IN NEW YORK CITY, TO HIS WIFE IN IRELAND, JANUARY 25, 1818.

Source: Journal of the American Irish Historical Society, XII (1912), 197-204.

. . . Oh, how long the days, how cheerless and fatiguing the nights since I parted with my Fanny and my little angel. Sea sickness, nor the toils of the ocean, nor the starvation which I suffered, nor the constant apprehension of our crazy old vessel going to the bottom, for ten tedious weeks, could ever wear me to the pitch it has if my mind was easy about you. But when the recollection of you and of my little Ned rushes on my mind with a force irresistible, I am amazed and confounded to think of the coolness with which I used to calculate on parting with my little family even for a day, to come to this strange country, which is the grave of the reputations, the morals, and of the lives of so many of our countrymen and countrywomen . . . .

We were safely landed in Philadelphia on the 7th of October and I had not so much as would pay my passage in a boat to take me ashore . . . I, however, contrived to get over, and . . . It was not long until I made out my father, whom I instantly knew, and no one could describe our feelings when I made myself known to him, and received his embraces, after an absence of seventeen years. [The father was a United Irish refugee of 1798]. . . The morning after landing I went to work to the printing . . . I think a journeyman printer's wages might be averaged at 7 1/2 dollars a week all the year round . . . . I worked in Philadelphia five and one-half weeks and saved 6 pounds, that is counting four dollars to the pound; in the currency of the United States the dollar is worth five shillings Irish . . . I found the printing and bookbinding overpowered with hands in New York. I remained idle for twelve days in consequence; when finding there was many out of employment like myself I determined to turn myself to something else, seeing that there was nothing to be got by idleness . . . . I was engaged by a bookseller to hawk maps for him at 7 dollars a week . . . . I now had about 60 dollars of my own saved . . . these I laid out in the purchase of pictures on New Year's Day, which I sell ever since. I am doing astonishingly well, thanks be to God, and was able on the 16th of this month to make a deposit of 100 dollars in the bank of the United States.

As yet it's only natural I should feel lonesome in this country, ninety-nine out of every hundred who come to it are at first disappointed . . Still, it's a fine country and a much better place for a poor man than Ireland . . . and much as they grumble at first, after a while they never think of leaving it. . . . One thing I think is certain, that if emigrants knew beforehand what they have to suffer for about the first six months after leaving home in every respect, they would never come here. However, an enterprising man, desirous of advancing himself in the world, will despise everything for coming to this free country, where a man is allowed to thrive and flourish without having a penny taken out of his pocket by government; no visits from tax gatherers, constables or soldiers, every one at liberty to act and speak as he likes, provided he does not hurt another, to slander and damn government, abuse public men in their office to their faces, wear your hat in court and smoke a cigar while speaking to the judge as familiarly as if he was a common mechanic, hundreds go unpunished for crimes for which they would be surely hung in Ireland; in fact they are so tender of life in this country that a person should have a very great interest to get himself hanged for anything.

A PROJECT FOR AN IRISH "FRONTIER" SETTLEMENT, 1818.

Source: Annals of Congress, Fifteenth Congress, First Session: Committee on Public Lands, February 16, 1818, pp. 201-2.

The memorial of the New York Irish Emigrant Association respectfully showeth: that your memorialists, while they presume most respectfully to direct your attention to the helpless and suffering condition of the numerous foreigners, who, flying from a complicated mass of want and misery, daily seek an asylum in the bosom of the United States, are emboldened by the recollection that a liberal encouragement to the settlement of meritorious strangers has always characterized the government and constituted authorities of the Union. The wise and brave founders of its independence held out to the oppressed and suffering of every nation the consoling assurance that in this country, at least, they should find a refuge and a home. The successors of these illustrious men have continued to redeem, in calmer and happier times, the pledge made to philosophy and benevolence amidst perilous scenes of distress and difficulty. From this humane and beneficent policy America has reaped a rich and happy harvest. She has added to the natural resources, the moral and physical strength to be derived from so many thousands and tens of thousands, who, actuated by attachment to her free Constitution, have adopted the nation where liberty has made and is making her most glorious stand, as the country of their choice.

Your memorialists in addressing your honorable body need not seek to enforce by experiment the generally received maxim of political economy that the wealth and solidity of a nation consist in the number, the social comforts, and the productive industry of its people. In the dense and crowded States and under the existing governments of Europe, these sources of wealth and stability are not always found well combined. It frequently does not happen that the social comforts, or even the productive industry are proportioned to the number of the people. In the extended territory and scattered population of the United States, however, and under their free and blessed institutions, it is an unquestionable and important truth that every increase of inhabitants when wisely and judiciously distributed and settled, adds to the social comforts and productive industry of the whole, and that the excess of population, which can not be considered as giving stability to the various governments of Europe, if suffered or encouraged to settle here, would incalculably increase our wealth and strength. But that accession is doubly valuable which also brings to the common fund with a mass of laborious industry unalterable attachment to the laws and constitution of the country. And surely, to give a wise direction to that industry, and to secure by well-placed kindness that attachment, are among the noblest exercises of legislative authority.

Your memorialists beg leave respectfully to represent that at no period since the establishment of American independence have the people of Europe, particularly the laboring classes, discovered so great a disposition as at present to emigrate to the United States. But the people of Ireland, from the peculiar pressure under which that country has so long been placed, have flocked hither in the greatest number and, perhaps, under the most trying and necessitous circumstances. They come, indeed, not to return and carry back the profits of casual speculations, but to dedicate to the land of their hopes, their persons, their families, their posterity, their affections, their all.

It is, however, a truth, regretted by those who have the best means of observation, that, for want of guides to their steps and congenial homes, where all their honest energies might be called at once into activity, and their hardy enterprise turned to their own advantage as well as to the general good, they remain perplexed, undecided, and dismayed by the novelty and difficulty of their situations. They have fled from want and oppression -- they touch the soil of freedom and abundance, but the manna of the wilderness melts in their sight. Before they can taste the fruits of happy industry, the tempter too often presents to their lips the cup that turns man to brute, and the very enterprise which would have made the fields to blossom, make the cities groan. Individual benevolence can not reach this evil. Individuals may indeed solicit, but it belongs to the chosen guardians of the public weal to administer the cure. Nor is the misdirection of the destruction of the capabilities and industry of these Emigrants to be regretted only on its own account. The story of their blasted hopes and fortunes is transmitted back and retailed with malicious exaggeration. Others, possessing more abundant means, and more prudent habits, who have been accustomed to look with longing eyes to this free country and contrast its happiness with the present state of Europe, are discouraged and deterred by their sufferings and misfortunes; and thus a large amount of active population and wealth inclined to flow into and enrich the United States is dammed up at the fountain head. A serious consideration of these circumstances induce your memorialists to hope and most earnestly but respectfully to request in behalf of those whose interests they urge, that a portion of unsold land may be set apart or granted to trustees for the purpose of being settled by Emigrants from Ireland on an extended term of credit. The conditions of this grant your memorialists wish to be such as may give to the settlers its entire benefit and may exclude all private speculation in others. They also beg leave to suggest after contemplating the various uncultivated tracts which invite the labor of men, that a situation adapted for a settlement of that description might be found among the lands lately purchased in the Illinois Territory.

Your memorialists are fully sensible that many of the most persuasive arguments in favor of their application must be addressed, and will not be addressed in vain, to the benevolence and sympathies of the Legislature: but they also confidently appeal to its wisdom and patriotism. The lands to which they have alluded being frontier and remote are neither likely to be speedily exposed to sale, to be rendered by cultivation subservient to the general prosperity nor by settlement conducive to the general strength.

The portion which might be granted on an extended credit would probably be paid for almost as soon as if it had not been brought into the market before its regular time. During that time in which it would otherwise remain unproductive (and therefore unprofitable) thousands of families would have acquired opulence, would have benefited the country by its cultivation, by the establishment of schools, the opening of roads, and the other improvements of social and civilized life. They would form a nucleus around which a more abundant population would rapidly accumulate, and all the contingent lands would be largely increased in value. The small loss which might appear to be sustained by the suspension of interest on the credit (if it should have any existence) will be abundantly compensated by the money and labor that must be immediately expended on works of general utility which the convenience and necessities of the settlers will naturally induce them to accomplish. But who can calculate the physical or moral or even the pecuniary advantages in time of war of having such a strong and embattled frontier?

The Irish emigrant, cherished and protected by the Government of the United States, will find his attachment for their interest increase in proportion to the benefits he has received. He will love with enthusiasm the country that affords him the means of honorable and successful enterprise and permits him to enjoy unmolested and undiminished the fruits of his honest industry. Ingratitude is not the vice of Irishmen. Fully appreciating his comparative comforts and the source from whence they flow, he will himself cherish and inculcate in his children, an unalterable devotion to his adopted and their native country. Should hostilities approach her in that quarter, whether in the savage forms of the tomahawk or scalping knife, or with the deadlier weapons of civilized warfare the Irish settlers with their hardy sons will promptly repel the invasion, drive back the war upon the enemy, and give to an extended frontier security and repose.

Your memorialists, therefore, humbly pray your honorable body to receive and listen favorably to their application. And, as in duty bound, they will ever pray, etc. ---

On behalf of the New York Irish Emigrant Association: New York, December, 1817.

Thos. Addis Emmet, President.
Daniel McCormick, Vice-President.
James McBride, 2nd Vice-President.
Andrew Herris, Treasurer.
John W. Mulligan, Secretary.
William Sampson, Secretary.
Wm. J. Macneven.
Mat. L. Davis.
J. Chambers.
Thomas Kirk.
J. H. Doyle.
John R. Skiddes.
Robert Fox.
R. Swanton.
James Sterling.
Wm. Edgar, Jr.
Matthew Carroll.
John Mayhue.
John Heffeman.
Dennis McCarthy
James R. Mullany.

A JACKSONIAN APPEAL TO THE "IRISH VOTE" : DEMOCRATIC CAMPAIGN SONG OF 1832.

Source: Louisiana Advertiser (New Orleans), April 13, 1832.

A Song for St. Patrick's Day

An Irishman's son our President is,
And now, to explain it, we proudly declare,
The foes of old Ireland are no friends of his
By this token--he ne'er did their carcarcass spare!
He beat them and bothered them once on a day,
When in his brave ranks he had some of the greens;
When the laurels of Pakenham withered away,
In the smoke that surrounded the man of Orleans.

. . . .

IRISH-AMERICAN VICTIMS OF POLITICAL REPRISALS.

Source: Letter to the Editor in The Truth Teller (New York), November 24, 1832.

We the subscribers, natives of Ireland -- and adopted citizens of the United States -- have been in the employment of Hance and Brooks, carpenters, in the Sixth Ward for some time, and consider ourselves justifiable in stating that from the time we were in their employment -- and the usage received from them -- there could be no objection to our abilities as workmen or our conduct as men, until the event of the late election.

It is well known by a respectable portion of our fellow-citizens of both the 6th and 14th Wards, that the above carpenters were very active in the cause of the opposition in the late election in the said wards, and, for their over-reaching the bounds of prudence and discretion, got very roughly handled the second day of the election. Mr. T. C. Colt, foreman to the above firm, presented to the subscribers a set of opposition tickets each, and said to us, if we would go to the polls and vote these tickets, that each one should receive his wages for any time lost on that occasion; and we believe that such order could or would not originate with the foreman. The above tickets were indignantly refused by every man, as well as the proffer of wages, and our reply was that we should go to the polls and vote according to our consciences, and any time spent there we were willing to lose; for we would vote for "Old Hickory" -- the Man of the People! ! !

The conduct of the above employers was most materially altered towards us on the following morning, and language very unbecoming and unusual was resorted to by one of them particularly, who said that Irishmen should not be encouraged in this country, and that he would not have one of them about his premises -- that he would sooner have inferior workmen, if any others could not be obtained, than have an Irishman employed in future. The aforesaid Hance and Brooks were determined to be consistent, and they kept their word, for the next day they discharged from their employment every Irishman in the concern!

. . . . The above statement the subscribers can substantiate in a court of justice; and if necessary a more minute detail can be given of the harshness and tyranny displayed by the above employers towards us from the time of the declaration of our sentiments.

James Purcell, 213 Wooster St.
John Keenan, 75 James St.
Michael Donoghue, 124 Franklin St.
Thomas Huston, 578 Greenwich St.
Michael Forrestal, 65 Suffolk St.

New York, November 22, 1832.

AN IRISH-AMERICAN HUMANITARIAN, 1833.

Source: Mathew Carey, Appeal to the Wealthy of the Land. Philadelphia. 1833, pp. 3-7.

. . . . Should it appear, as it probably will, to some of my readers, that I have expressed myself with too much warmth, in discussing the sufferings of the seamstresses, etc., let it be borne in mind, that I have been pleading the cause of probably 12,000 women in Boston, New York, Philadelphia, and Baltimore (with souls as precious in the eye of heaven as the most exalted females that ever trod the earth -- as a Maria Theresa, a Princess Victoria, a Mrs. Washington, a Mrs. Madison, or a Mrs. Monroe) who are grievously oppressed and reduced to the utmost penury, in a land literally flowing with milk and honey, while many of those for whom they toil, make immense fortunes, by their labours.

We are assured, as I have stated, by ladies fully competent to judge on the subject, that nine cotton shirts a week are as much as the great mass of seamstresses can make. Those shirts are frequently made for 6, 8, and 10 cents, leaving 54, 72, and 90 cents a week for the incessant application of a human being, during thirteen or fourteen hours a day, for the payment of rent, the purchase of food, clothes, drink, soap, candles and fuel!

Deplorable as is the condition of the poor in the crowded cities of Europe, there are few females there who earn much less than this -- and therefore, it must follow, that there is frequently as intense a degree of distress suffered here, as in London or Paris. The principal difference is not in the intensity, but in the extent of the distress. Compared with London or Paris, there are few who suffer in this way here. But it is no alleviation of the misery of an unfortunate female in Philadelphia or Boston, who makes shirts for six or eight cents, or even ten, that is to say, who earns from nine to fifteen cents per day, that there are fewer similarly circumstanced here than in those cities.

It is often triumphantly asked, respecting the case of the women who are so very inadequately remunerated for their labours, what remedy can be applied to such an inveterate evil? Does not the proportion between supply and demand, in this, as in all other cases, regulate prices? And while there is such an overproportion of labour in the market, must not competition reduce prices, as it has done, to the lowest grade, even below the minimum necessary to support existence?

I am well aware of the superabundance of female labour -- of the direful effects of over-driven competition, not only on the comfort and happiness, but on the morals of the labouring classes of society, in every quarter of the globe. But I contend for it, that every principle of honour, justice, and generosity, forbids the employer to take advantage of the distress and wretchedness of those he employs, and cut down their wages below the minimum necessary to procure a sufficiency of plain food and clothes to guard against the inclemency of the weather. Whoever passes this line of demarcation, is guilty of the heinous offence of "grinding the faces of the poor." The labour of every human being ought to insure this remuneration at least. And I am persuaded that there are thousands of honourable men who give inadequate wages to males as well as females, merely because they have never thought sufficiently on the subject; and who, therefore, have no idea of the real state of the case. They would scorn to give the wages they do at present, were they aware of the distress and misery thus entailed on those by whose labours, I emphatically repeat, they not only enjoy all the comforts of life, but many of them make immense fortunes. My object is to induce upright men thus circumstanced, to scrutinize the affair, and obey the dictates of their better feelings as soon as they have ascertained the truth. Of the honourable issue I cannot entertain a doubt.

Let me most earnestly, but most respectfully, conjure the ladies, into whose hands these lines may come, to ponder deeply, and frequently, and lastingly, on the deplorable condition of so many many of their sex, who are ground to the earth by an inadequate remuneration for their painful labours. Let them raise their voices, and exert their influence in their defence, and urge their male friends to enter the lists in the holy cause of suffering humanity. I am not so enthusiastic or deluded as to suppose that a complete remedy can be applied to so enormous and so inveterate an evil -- an evil, the remedy of which requires more generosity and disinterestedness than usually fall to the lot of mankind. But by proper efforts, the oppression of the mass of the sufferers may at least be mitigated, and no inconsiderable portion of them may be completely relieved.

The ladies will, I hope, pardon me for an observation which applies to some of them, but I hope to only a few. I have known a lady expend a hundred dollars on a party; pay thirty or forty dollars for a bonnet, and fifty for a shawl; and yet make a hard bargain with a seamstress or washerwoman, who had to work at her needle or at the washing-tub for thirteen or fourteen hours a day to make a bare livelihood for herself and a numerous family of small children! This is "a sore oppression under the sun," and ought to be eschewed by every honourable mind. "Let it be reformed altogether.". . .

. . .My object is to consider the case of those whose services are so inadequately remunerated, owing to the excess of labour beyond the demand for it, that they can barely support themselves while in good health and fully employed; and, of course, when sick or unemployed, must perish, unless relieved by charitable individuals, benevolent societies, or the guardians of the poor. I use the word "perish" with due deliveration, and a full conviction of its appropriate application to the case, however revolting it may seem to the reader; for as these people depend for daily support on their daily or weekly wages, they are, when those wages are stopped by whatever means, utterly destitute of wherewith to support their existence, and actually become paupers, and therefore, without the aid above stated, would, I repeat, "perish" of want.

The crisis of suffering through which this class about three years since passed there and elsewhere, and the occurrence of similar suffering in all hard winters (and, in other seasons, from sickness and destitution of employment), often without receiving that extra aid which such a state of things loudly demands, appears to require a sober and serious investigation, in order to probe to the bottom so deplorable a state of things, whereby the comfort and happiness of such a large portion of human beings are so cruelly shipwrecked, and to ascertain what are the causes of the evil, and whether it be susceptible of any remedy.

The erroneous opinions to which I have alluded are --

1. That every man, woman, and grown child, able and willing to work may find employment.

2. That the poor, by industry, prudence, and economy, may at all times support themselves comfortably, without depending on eleemosynary aid -- and, as a corollary from these positions,

3. That their sufferings and distresses chiefly, if not wholly, arise from their idleness, their dissipation, and their extravagance.

4. That taxes for the support of the poor, and aid afforded them by charitable individuals, or benevolent societies, are pernicious, as, by encouraging the poor to depend on them, they foster their idleness and improvidence, and thus produce, or at least increase, the poverty and distress they are intended to relieve.

These opinions, so far as they have operated -- and, through the mischievous zeal and industry of the school of political economists by which they have been promulgated, they have spread widely -- have been pernicious to the rich and the poor. They tend to harden the hearts of the former against the sufferings and distresses of the latter -- and of course prolong those sufferings and distresses.

"Posterity will scarcely credit the extent to which the popular feeling has been worked upon and warped by the ravings of some of our modern economists. They, truly, have done all that in them lay, TO EXTINGUISH IN THE BOSOMS OF THE MORE OPULENT CLASSES, EVERY SPARK OF GENEROUS AND BENEVOLENT FEELING TOWARDS THE DESTITUTE AND NEEDY PAUPER. In their eyes, pauperism is a crime, for which nothing short of absolute starvation can form an adequate punishment." -- London Quarterly Review, July, 1828.

Many wealthy individuals, benevolent and liberal, apprehensive lest by charitable aid to persons in distress, they might produce evil to society, are, by these pernicious and cold-blooded doctrines, prevented from indulging the feelings of their hearts, and employing a portion of their superfluous wealth for the best purpose to which it can be appropriated -- that purpose which, at the hour of death, will afford the most solid comfort on retrospection -- that is, "to feed the hungry; to give drink to the thirsty; to clothe the naked; to comfort the comfortless." The economists in question, when they are implored by the starving poor for "bread", tender them "a stone." To the unfeeling and uncharitable of the rich (and such unhappily there are), these doctrines afford a plausible pretext, of which they are not slow to avail themselves, for withholding their aid from the poor. They have moreover tended to attach a sort of disrepute to those admirable associations of ladies and gentlemen, for the relief of the poor, on which Heaven looks down with complacence, and which form a delightful oasis in the midst of the arid deserts of sordid selfishness which on all sides present themselves to the afflicted view of the contemplative observer . . . .

The higher orders of society have generally enjoyed the advantages of a good education and good examples: the censorial eye of the public is on them, and serves as a curb to restrain them from guilt: regard to character has a powerful operation. Nevertheless, do we not unfortunately see considerable numbers of them who lapse from the paths of rectitude? How powerfully do such lapses tend to extenuate those of the poor, who are under no such controlling or restraining circumstances, and have so much stronger incentives to aberration!

The population of Philadelphia is about 160,000 souls, of whom about 100,000 depend on the labour of their hands; 40,000 are probably laborers, hodmen, seamstresses, families of workmen on the canals and rail-roads. The utmost industry and economy they can employ will scarcely suffice to sustain them, if not unremittingly employed; and few of them are so fortunate as to be employed through the year. These last descriptions of persons are those whose case I have undertaken to consider.

Philadelphia, June 20, 1833

Report on the Destruction of the Ursuline Convent, August 11, 1834

Source: Documents Relating to the Ursuline Convent in Charlestown, Massachusetts, Boston, 1842, pp. 16-17.

. . . The fact that the dwelling of inoffensive females and children, guiltless of wrong to the persons, property, or reputation of others, and reposing in fancied security under the protection of the law, has been thus assaulted by a riotous mob, and ransacked, plundered, and burnt to the ground, and its terrified inmates, in the dead hour of night, driven from their beds into the fields; and that this should be done within the limits of one of the most populous towns of the commonwealth, and in the midst of an assembled multitude of spectators; that the perpetrators should have been engaged for seven hours or more in the work of destruction, with hardly an effort to prevent or arrest them; that many of them should afterwards be so far sheltered or protected by public sympathy or opinion, as to render the ordinary means of detection ineffectual; and that the sufferers are entitled to no legal redress from the public, for the outrage against their persons and destruction of their property, is an event of fearful import as well as of the profoundest shame and humiliation.

It has come upon us like the shock of the earthquake, and has disclosed a state of society and public sentiment of which we believe no man was before aware.

If for the purpose of destroying a person, or family, or institution, it be only necessary to excite a public prejudice, by the dissemination of falsehoods and criminal accusations, and under its sanction to array a mob; and there be neither an efficient magistracy nor a sense of public duty or justice sufficient for its prevention, and if property may be thus sacrificed without the possibility of redress, who among us is safe?

The cry may be of bigotry to-day and heresy to-morrow; of public usurpation at one time, and private oppression at another; or any other of those methods by which the ignorant, the factious, and the desperate, may be excited; and the victim may be sacrificed without protection or relief.

It is hoped that the fearful warning thus suddenly given, enforced as it is by siminar occurrences in other states, will arrest the public attention; check the prevailing disposition to give credence to injurious and calumnious reports; will produce throughout the country a higher sense of the qualifications requisite for magisterial office; and lead to amendments and improvements of our laws, which are thus found so sadly defective.

And above all, may it rebuke the spirit of intolerance thus unexpectedly developed, so fatal to the genius of our institutions, and unrestrained, so fatal to their continuance. If there be one feeling which more than any other should pervade this country, composing, as it were, the atmosphere of social life, it is that of enlightened toleration, comprehending all within the sphere of its benevolence, and extending over all the shield of mutual protection.

IRISH AMERICAN REACTION TO THE CHARLESTOWN CONVENT INCIDENT, 1834.

Source: Boston Commercial Gazette, August 13, 1834.

Fears were entertained yesterday that there would be fresh disturbances last evening. It was reported that the Irish labourers on the Worcester, Lowell, and Providence railroads were on their way to the city, in great numbers, for the purpose of aiding their Irish brethren in avenging the insult that was offered to them by the destruction of the Catholic seminary at Charlestown. It is true, we believe, that several hundred of these labourers arrived in this city last evening; but we have heard of no acts of violence on their part, or from any other quarter. The evening passed off quietly, at least so far as this city is concerned, although the streets were thronged until a late hour. We have rarely seen so many people abroad as there was last evening.

Much credit is due to Bishop Fenwick, for the exertions he made to dissuade the Catholics from all acts of retaliatory violence. He dispatched five or six priests in different directions during the afternoon, to intercept the labourers who were known to be on their way to Boston, and instruct them not to raise a finger in defence of what they consider their violated rights. This was a judicious movement, considering the unparalleled state of excitement into which our citizens have been suddenly thrown, by the outrageous conduct of a portion of the people of Cambridge and Charlestown.

We understand that all the Independent Light Infantry Companies were under arms last night, prepared with ball cartridges to act in any emergency which might require their services. Hundreds of respectable citizens were also "on hand," to aid the civil and military authorities. Most sincerely do we hope that there may be no occasion for them to act.

PROTESTANT COMMENDATION FOR THE BISHOP

So great was the excitement among the Catholics yesterday that Bishop Fenwick deemed it necessary to call them together in the afternoon, at the church in Franklin street. At 6 o'clock, several hundred were assembled, when the Bishop came in and addressed them for about thirty minutes in a most eloquent and judicious manner. He deserves the warmest commendation from his Protestant fellow-citizens for the admirable style in which he managed this business. Previous to speaking, the Bishop read a part of the fifth chapter of Matthew, containing the following among other verses:

"You have heard that it hath been said, and eye for an eye, and a tooth for a tooth. But I say to your, not to resist evil, but if one strike thee on thy right cheek, turn to him also the other:

"And if a man will contend with thee in judgment, and take away thy coat, let go thy cloak also unto him. And whosoever will force thee one mile, go with him other two.

"You have heard that it hath been said, Thou shalt love thy neighbor and hate thy enemy. But I say to you, love your enemies, do good to them that hate; and pray for them that persecute and calumniate you."

Bishop Fenwick then proceeded to address his hearers, embracing several hundred of both sexes. He spoke of the destruction of the Ursuline Convent and adjacent buildings. He spoke also of the beauty and utility of that institution, and alluded to its growing popularity among the intelligent classes, both in this vicinity and at a distance. Among the pupils of the institution were some from Louisiana, and the West India Islands. After denouncing the conduct of the incendiaries in appropriate terms, he asked "What is to be done? Shall we say to our enemies, you have destroyed our buildings, and we will destroy yours? No, my brethren, this is not the religion of Jesus Christ -- this is not in accordance with the spirit of that blessed religion we all profess. Turn not a finger in your own defefence, and there are those around you who will see that justice is done you."

The Bishop then complimented the City Authorities and others for the stand they had taken in defense of the rights of the Catholics; and he assured his hearers that they had the sympathies of all respectable citizens. The destruction of the Convent, he said, was an act of the most degraded of the human species, and it met with no favour from the intelligent people of Boston. He impressed upon the minds of his Catholic brethren the fact that it was not their duty to seek revenge for this vile act; and said that that man was an enemy to the religion he professed, and would put the Catholic Church in jeopardy, who should raise a finger against their opponents at this time.

The Bishop said he had no fears that those who were present would act in opposition to his advice; and if any acts of violence were committed, it would be by those who, with, perhaps, a commendable ardour and alacrity were rushing to their aid from a distance, and who may not have correct information on the subject. He enjoined it upon all present as a solemn duty to inform these individuals -- if they should fall in with any of them -- of what he had said, and the advice he had just given them.

AN IRISH-AMERICAN SPOKESMAN FOR JACKSONIAN DEMOCRACY, 1837

Source: John L. O'Sullivan, "Introduction," The United States Magazine and Democratic Review, Vol. I, No. 1 (October, 1837), pp. 2-11.

The Democratic Principle

We believe, then, in the principle of democratic republicanism, in its strongest and purest sense. We have an abiding confidence in the virtue, intelligence, and full capacity for self-government, of the great mass of our people -- our industrious, honest, manly, intelligent millions of freemen.

We are opposed to all self-styled "wholesome restraints" on the free action of the popular opinion and will, other than those which have for their sole object the prevention of precipitate legislation. This latter object is to be attained by the expedient of the division of power, and by causing all legislation to pass through the ordeal of successive forms; to be sifted through the discussions of coordinate legislative branches, with mutual suspensive veto powers. Yet all should be dependent with equal directness and promptness on the influence of public opinion; the popular will should be equally the animating and moving spirit of them all, and ought never to find in any of its own creatures a self-imposed power, capable (when misused either by corrupt ambition or honest error) of resisting itself, and defeating its own determined object. We cannot, therefore, look with an eye of favor on any such forms of representation as, by length of tenure of delegated power, tend to weaken that universal and unrelaxing responsibility to the vigilance of public opinion, which is the true conservative principle of our institutions.

The great question here occurs, which is of vast importance to this country (was it not once near dissolving the Union, and plunging it into the abyss of civil war?) -- of the relative rights of majorities and minorities. Though we go for the republican principle of the supremacy of the will of the majority, we acknowledge, in general, a strong sympathy with minorities, and consider that their rights have a high moral claim on the respect and justice of majorities; a claim not always fairly recognized in practice by the latter, in the full sway of power, when flushed with triumph, and impelled by strong interests. This has ever been the point of the democratic cause most open to assault, and most difficult to defend.

This difficulty does not arise from any intrinsic weakness. The democratic theory is perfect and harmonious in all its parts; and if this point is not so self-evidently clear as the rest is generally, in all candid discussion, conceded to be, it is because of certain false principles of government, which have, in all practical experiments of the theory, been interwoven with the democratic portions of the system, being borrowed from the example of anti-democratic systems of government. We shall always be willing to meet this question frankly and fairly. The great argument against pure democracy, drawn from this source, is this:

Though the main object with reference to which all social institutions ought to be modelled is undeniably, as stated by the democrat, "the greatest good of the greatest number," yet it by no means follows that the greatest number always rightly understands its own greatest good. Highly pernicious error has often possessed the minds of nearly a whole nation; while the philosopher in his closet, and an enlightened few about him, powerless against the overwhelming current of popular prejudice and excitement, have alone possessed the truth, which the next generation may perhaps recognise and practice, though its author, now sainted, has probably in his own time, been its martyr. The original adoption of the truth would have saved perhaps oceans of blood, and mountains of misery and crime.

How much stronger, then, the case against the absolute supremacy of the opinion and will of the majority, when its numerical preponderance is, as often happens, comparatively small. And if the larger proportion of the more wealthy and cultivated classes of the society are found on the side of the minority, the disinterested observer may well be excused if he hesitate long before he awards the judgment, in a difficult and complicated question, in favor of the mere numerical argument. Majorities are often as liable to error of opinion, and not always free from a similar proneness to selfish abuse of power, as minorities; and a vast amount of injustice may often be perpetrated, and consequent general social injury be done, before the evil reaches that extreme at which it rights itself by revolution, moral or physical.

We have here, we believe, correctly stated the anti-democratic side of the argument on this point. It is not to be denied that it possesses something more than plausibility. It has certainly been the instrument of more injury to the cause of the democratic principle than all the bayonets and cannon that have ever been arrayed in support of it against that principle. The inference from it is, that the popular opinion and will must not be trusted with the supreme and absolute direction of the general interests; that it must be subjected to the "conservative checks" of minority interests, and to the regulation of the "more enlightened wisdom" of the "better classes," and those to whom the possession of a property "test of merit" gives what they term "a stake in the community." And here we find ourselves in the face of the great stronghold of the anti-democratic, or aristocratic, principle.

It is not our purpose, in this place, to carry out the discussion of this question. The general scope and tendency of the present work are designed to be directed towards the refutation of this sophistical reasoning and inference. It will be sufficient here to allude to the leading ideas by which they are met by the advocate of the pure democratic cause.

In the first place, the greatest number are more likely, at least, as a general rule, to understand and follow their own greatest good, than is the minority.

In the second, a minority is much more likely to abuse power for the promotion of its own selfish interests, at the expense of the majority of numbers -- the substantial and producing mass of the nation -- than the latter is to oppress unjustly the former. The social evil is also, in that case, proportionately greater. This is abundantly proved by the history of all aristocratic interests that have existed, in various degrees and modification, in the world. A majority cannot subsist upon a minority; while the natural, and in fact uniform, tendency of a minority entrusted with governmental authority is, to surround itself with wealth, splendor, and power, at the expense of the producing mass, creating and perpetuating those artificial social distinctions which violate the natural equality of rights of the human race, and at the same time offend and degrade the true dignity of human nature.

In the third place, there does not naturally exist any such original superiority of a minority class above the great mass of a community, in intelligence and competence for the duties of government -- even putting out of view its constant tendency to abuse from selfish motives and the safer honesty of the mass. The general diffusion of education; the facility of access to every species of knowledge important to the great interests of the community; the freedom of the press, whose very licentiousness cannot materially impair its permanent value, in this country at least, make the pretensions of those self-styled "better classes" to the sole possession of the requisite intelligence for the management of public affairs, too absurd to be entitled to any other treatment than an honest, manly contempt.

As far as superior knowledge and talent confer on their possessor a natural charter of privilege to control his associates, and exert an influence on the direction of the general affairs of the community, the free and natural action of that privilege is best secured by a perfectly free democratic system, which will abolish all artificial distinctions, and, preventing the accumulation of any social obstacles to advancement, will permit the free development of every germ of talent, wherever it may chance to exist, whether on the proud mountain summit, in the humble valley, or by the wayside of common life.

But the question is not yet satisfactorily answered, how the relation between majorities and minorities, in the frequent case of a collision of sentiments and particular interests, is to be so adjusted as to secure a mutual respect of rights, to preserve harmony and good will, and save society from the *malum extremum discordia*, from being as a house divided against itself -- and thus to afford free scope to that competition, discussion, and mutual moral influence, which cannot but result, in the end, in the ascendancy of the truth, and in "the greatest good of the greatest number."

On the one side, it has only been shown that the absolute government of the majority does not always afford a perfect guarantee against the misuse of its numerical power over the weakness of the minority. On the other, it has been shown that this chance of misuse is, as a general rule, far less than in the opposite relation of the ascendancy of a minority; and that the evils attendant upon it are infinitely less, in every point of view, in the one case than the other. But this is not yet a complete or satisfactory solution of the problem. Have we but a choice of evils? Is there, then, such a radical deficiency in the moral elements implanted by its Creator in human society, that no other alternative can be devised by which both evils shall be avoided, and a result attained more analogous to the beautiful and glorious harmony of the rest of his creation?

It were scarcely consistent with a true and living faith in the existence and attributes of that Creator, so to believe; and such is not the democratic belief. The reason of the plausibility with which appeal may be made to the experience of so many republics, to sustain this argument against democratic institutions, is, that the true theory of national self-government has been hitherto but imperfectly understood; bad principles have been mixed up with the good; and the republican government has been administered on ideas and in a spirit borrowed from the strong governments of the other forms; and to the corruptions and manifold evils which have never failed, in the course of time, to evolve themselves out of these seeds of destruction, is ascribable the eventual failure of those experiments, and the consequent doubt and discredit which have attached themselves to the democratic principles on which they were, in the outset, mainly based.

It is under the word government, that the subtle danger lurks. Understood as a central consolidated power, managing and directing the various general interest of the society, all government is evil, and the parent of evil. A strong and active democratic government, in the common sense of the term, is an evil, differing only in degree and mode of operation, and not in nature, from a strong despotism. This difference is certainly vast, yet, inasmuch as these strong governmental powers must be wielded by human agents, even as the powers of the despotism, it is, after all, only a difference in degree; and the tendency to demoralization and tyranny is the same, though the development of the evil results is much more gradual and slow in the one case than in the other.

Hence the demagogue -- hence the faction -- hence the mob -- hence the violence, licentiousness, and instability -- hence the ambitious struggles of parties and their leaders for power-- hence the abuses of that power by majorities and their leaders -- hence the indirect oppressions of the general by partial interests -- hence (fearful symptom) the demoralization of the great men of the nation, and of the nation itself, proceeding (unless checked in time by the more healthy and patriotic portion of the mind of the nation rallying itself to reform the principles and sources of the evil) gradually to that point of maturity at which relief from the tumult of moral and physical confusion is to be found only under the shelter of an energetic armed despotism.

The best government is that which governs least. No human depositories can, with safety, be trusted with the power of legislation upon the general interests of society so as to operate directly or indirectly on the industry and property of the community. Such power must be perpetually liable to the most pernicious abuse, from the natural imperfection, both in wisdom of judgment and purity of purpose, of all human legislation, exposed consistently to the pressure of partial interests; interests which, at the same time that they are essentially selfish and tyrannical, are ever vigilant, persevering, and subtle in all the arts of deception and corruption. In fact, the whole history of human society and government may be safely appealed to, in evidence that the abuse of such power a thousand fold more than overbalances its beneficial use.

Legislation has been the fruitful parent of nine-tenths of all the evil, moral and physical, by which mankind has been afflicted since the creation of the world, and by which human nature has been self-degraded, fettered, and oppressed. Government should have as little as possible to do with the general business and interests of the people. If it once undertake these functions as its rightful province of action, it is impossible to say to it "thus far shalt thou go, and no farther." It will be impossible to confine it to the public interests of the commonwealth. It will be perpetually tampering with private interests, and sending forth seeds of corruption which will result in the demoralization of the society. Its domestic action should be confined to the administration of justice, for the protection of the natural equal rights of the citizen, and the preservation of social order. In all other respects, the VOLUNTARY PRINCIPLE, the principle of FREEDOM, suggested to us by the analogy of the divine government of the Creator, and already recognised by us with perfect success in the great social interest of Religion, affords the true "golden rule" which is alone abundantly competent to work out the best possible general result of order and happiness from that chaos of characters, ideas, motives, and interests -- human society . . . .

This principle, therefore, constitutes our "point of departure." It has never yet received any other than a very partial and imperfect application to practice among men, all human society having been hitherto perpetually chained down to the ground by myriads of lilliputian fetters of artificial government and prescription. Nor are we yet prepared for its full adoption in this country. Far, very far indeed, from it; yet is our gradual tendency toward it clear and sure . . . .

We deem it scarcely necessary to say that we are opposed to all precipitate radical changes in social institutions. Adopting "Nature she accomplishes her most mighty results of the good and beautiful by the silent and slow operation of great principles, without the convulsions of too rapid action . . . .

We are willing to make every reform in our institutions that may be commended by the test of the democratic principle -- to democratize them-but only so rapidly as shall appear, to the most cautious wisdom, consistent with a due regard to the existing development of public opinion and to the permanence of the progress made. Every instance in which the action of government can be simplified, and one of the hundred giant arms curtailed, with which it now stretches around its fatal protecting grasp over almost all the various interests of society, to substitute the truly healthful action of the free voluntary principle -- every instance in which the operation of the public opinion and will, fairly signified, can be brought to bear more directly upon the action of delegated powers -- we would regard as so much gained for the true interest of the society and of mankind at large. In this path we cannot go wrong; it is only necessary to be cautious not to go too fast . . . .

For Democracy is the cause of Humanity. It has faith in human nature. It believes in its essential equality and fundamental goodness. It respects, with a solemn reverence to which the proudest artificial institutions and distinctions of society have no claim, the human soul. It is the cause of philanthropy. Its object is to emancipate the mind of the mass of men from the degrading and disheartening fetters of social distinctions and advantages; to bid it walk abroad through the free creation "in its own majesty"; to war against all fraud, oppression, and violence; by striking at their root, to reform all the infinitely varied human misery which has grown out of the old and false ideas by which the world has been so long misgoverned; to dismiss the hireling soldier; to spike the cannon, and bury the bayonet; to burn the gibbet, and open the debtor's dungeon; to substitute harmony and mutual respect for the jealousies and discord now subsisting between different classes of society, as the consequence of their artificial classification. It is the cause of Christianity, to which a slight allusion has been already made . . . . And that portion of the peculiar friends and ministers of religion who now, we regret to say, cast the weight of their social influence against the cause of democracy, under the false prejudice of an affinity between it and infidelity (no longer, in this century, the case, and which, in the last, was but a consequence of the overgrown abuses of religion found, by the reforming spirit that then awakened in Europe, in league with despotism), understand but little either its true spirit, or that of their own faith.

It is, moreover, a cheerful creed, a creed of high hope and universal love, noble and ennobling; while all others, which imply a distrust of mankind, and of the natural moral principles infused into it by its Creator, for its own self-development and self-regulation, are as gloomy and selfish, in the tone of moral sentiment which pervades them, as they are degrading in their practical tendency, and absurd in theory, when examined by the light of original principles . . . .

AN EDITORIAL TO IRISH EMIGRANTS

Source: The Truth Teller, New York, August 31, 1839.

We have ever deemed it a matter of obligation as well as a source of pleasure at all times to raise our voice of counsel and caution for the protection of the Irish Emigrant, and the direction of his wandering footsteps in an unknown and foreign land to those places where his habits of unsuspecting honesty and native industry are most likely to receive their just appreciation and best reward, and where the least peril to health exists from the general prevalence of disease or the periodical afflictions of peculiar localities.

We hope most confidently that the day is not distant when the ample, but now scattered rays of humanity, patriotism, and spirit will be forced by the constantly growing necessity of the case to converge their united strength upon this important point, and shed the broad and durable light of disinterested counsel upon the inexperienced mind of the hapless exile in the laborious pursuit of happiness in foreign climes, and save him from human wolves which are ever on the alert to pounce upon him as their fittest victim.

We indulge in these remarks in the hope that they may have some weight with our intelligent and reasonable citizens, both native and adopted, inducing them to unite in forming some solid, comprehensive, and benevolent measure which would meet the poor emigrant's necessities upon reaching our free and hospitable shores, and prevent him from falling an easy prey to the first specious friend or insidious imposter which infests our wharves.

We give the following information with pleasure, for the benefit of emigrants and others wanting permanent employment. The Legislature of Pennsylvania have made a recent and liberal appropriation for the prosecution of the "North Branch Canal." This canal will not be completed in less than three years, and runs through perhaps the healthiest region of country in the Union. It commences at the mouth of the Lackawana in Lucerne county, and terminates at Tioga Point, near the state line in Bradford county. Five hundred men will find employment at this work at $1.12 1/2 per day. The cheapest and shortest route from New York is by Newark, Morristown, and Carbondale, and from the northern part of Pennsylvania or New York, by Tioga Point, Bradford County, The most numerous Catholic settlement in Pennsylvania is in the vicinity of this work . . . . Rev. Mr. Fitzsimmons is the pastor of Carbondale, on the way from New York, fifteen miles from the Lucerne division of the Canal. . . . Rev. Mr. O'Reily is pastor of Silverdale and the Towanda division. This is mentioned for the benefit of the labourer, as they are zealous and anxious to extend to emigrants and all others soliciting it the most accurate information in relation to the honesty or dishonesty of the several contractors on this immense work.

These Revd. gentlemen always feel it an important portion of their pastoral care to warn their countrymen against the immoral contractor, who distributes among his labourers the fatal draft of ardent poison for the unmanly purpose of working his unfortunate victims beyond their natural strength, and of weakening, during the delirious excitement which follows the maddening libation . . . [their] reason . . . at . . . the time most seduously selected for the settlement of accounts. . . . Such an evil can well be avoided by consulting these clergymen and others of similar benevolence and humanity.

AN IRISH-AMERICAN REFORMER, 1841

Source: Report in Favor of the Abolition of Capital Punishment made in the Legislature of the State of New York, Albany, 1841, pp. 138-9. O'Sullivan was chairman of the committee on capital punishment, and wrote its report.

Abolition of Capital Punishment --- John L. O'Sullivan

. . . . . The committee concluded this topic, therefore, by the reassertion, with a fearless challenge of disproof, of the conviction already above stated, that the executioner is the indirect cause of more murders and more deaths, than he ever punishes or avenges. In relation to the powerful bearing of this solemn truth upon the question under discussion, they feel that it cannot be necessary for the many more fully to enlarge.

Nor is it an untried experiment on which it is here proposed to enter. Other communities, when in a stage of civilization, and of general moral culture, far inferior to that which invites us now no longer to delay in following their example, have abolished the punishment of death -- and with such a success as amply to justify us in the great reform proposed by the committee. If it can be shown that a single community has ever existed, which has been able to sustain itself against the dangers apprehended by the opponents of this reform -- whose statute-books have been kept pure from the hideous stain of blood which it is our object now to erase from ours, and where the life of the citizen and the general order and security of the society have yet been not less safe than they are ever made by the presumed protection of the penalty of death -- the sole ground will be swept away on which the great public crime of its continuance can be even attempted to be palliated, this ground of a supposed "social necessity." . . .

The history of all human progress is but a record of the slow and successive conquests of reason over error. The strongest resistance which the latter makes is always derived from a similar appeal to the authority of venerable antiquity. All civilizations have had their birth in barbarism; and hence the long and obstinate retention by the former of many of the habits and ideas which were a disgrace even to the latter. It is not in this country -- happily for us in a thousand ways -- that such argument as this will avail much, to turn back our hand from any good work of reform to which we are prompted, alike by that Christianity which brings us a direct revelation of the will of the great Author of our being, and by that Reason which interprets to us that same will from the evidences of experience and the philosophy of our own wonderful nature. And often and sadly as the steps of mankind may have been led astray by the sole, unaided guidance of the latter, we need never hesitate to resign ourselves fearlessly to it whenever we find it, as we so signally do in the present case, illustrated and confirmed by the former.

We have gone on gradually restricting more and more the application of the punishment of death, which in the country from which we derived the main bulk of our law embraced at the commencement of the present century not less than 300 offences, and still includes a large number to which we should be shocked at the thought of again extending it.

These successive ameliorations of our penal law have been attended with such good effect, that no proposition has ever been advanced to retrace any one of these steps. What reason can we have to doubt that the completion of this holy reform, by abolishing the punishment of death from the last few applications at which it still lingers, will be attended with equally satisfactory results -- especially with all the encouragement afforded us in the practice of the experiment wherever and whenever it has hitherto been tried? Let us, at least for consistency's sake, either restore it to the other offences for which we have abolished it, if it be indeed an efficacious restraint upon their perpetration; or if such is not the case -- if the punishment of death has been found to be not only useless, but worse than useless, for that purpose, in its application to those offences -- let us carry out the same progressive reform to its legitimate consummation, and erase from our statute-book the last vestige of a policy worthy only of the barbarism in which it had its origin . . . .

The committee repeat in conclusion, that they are satisfied that the time is now ripe, full ripe, for the consummation of the great and noble reform in the practice of our penal justice, which they have endeavored to discuss in the preceding pages . . . . A very large majority of the people of this State are at heart decidedly opposed to capital punishment -- that the number would be exceedingly small who would not hail with high gratification at least the trial of the proposed reform as an experiment, an experiment that may be with perfect ease abandoned by the next or any succeeding Legislature -- and that after the attention which has been drawn to the subject at the present session, a very profound dissatisfaction and disappointment would pervade the public mind, if any causes were allowed by this body to frustrate or delay a definite action upon it. It behooves and will well become the State of New York to take the initiative in this wise and sacred philanthropy -- the State from whose example and lead have already proceeded two of the most important popular and legal reforms that have made, and are rapidly making, their way, far and wide, throughout both her sister States in this great republican Union, and even the nations separated from us by three thousand miles of ocean, the great Temperance Reform and the Abolition of Imprisonment for Debt -- the State, too, that has given birth to many a noble son who have advocated this reform, of whom two alone need here be referred to, a Tompkins and a Livingston; and to whose memories no worthier monument, than the proposed law, could be erected by a proud and grateful country.

In accordance with the views herein above expressed, the committee asks leave to introduce a bill and a concurrent resolution.

All which is respectfully submitted, by the unanimous direction of the committee.

NEW YORK'S TRIBUTE TO THE MEMORY OF DANIEL O'CONNELL, 1847

Source: Circular printed in New York City, June 1847.

SPECIAL ORDERS

The Societies composing the Funeral Procession in memory of DANIEL O'CONNELL, will form on the 22nd instant, at 9 o'clock precisely, in the following manner, in double ranks: --

ASSIGNMENT OF POSITIONS.

Society No. 1 will form on the West side of Second Avenue, right resting on Tenth-street.

" No. 2 " " " " " " " " " right resting on left of No. 1, at Eleventh street, left running to Fourteenth-street, cross Fourteenth-street to East side of the Avenue, and down the Avenue to Tenth-street, and left down Tenth street.

" No. 3 will form on the Avenue, right on Tenth-street, left extending down to and in Ninth-street to East River.

" No. 4 will form on the Avenue, right on Ninth-street, left down to and in Eighth-street.

" No. 5 will form in Eighth-street, right on Second Avenue, left down to East River.

" No. 6 will form on the Avenue, right on Eighth Street, left down to and in Seventh-street to East River.

" No. 7 will form on the Avenue, right on Seventh-street., left down to and in Sixth street to East River.

" No. 8 will form on the Avenue, right on Sixth-street, left down to Fifth-street.

" No. 9 will form in Fifth-street, right on Second Avenue, left down to East River.

" No. 10 will form in Fifth street, right on left of No. 9.

" No. 11 will form on Second Avenue, right on Fifth-street, left down to and in Fourth-street.

" No. 12 will form on Second Avenue, right on Fourth street, left down to and in Third-street.

" No. 13 will form on Third-street, left extending to East River.

" No. 14 will form on Second Avenue, right on Third-street, down to Second-street.

" No. 15 will form on Second-street, right on Second Avenue down to East River.

" No. 16 will form on Second Avenue, right on Second-street down to First-street.

" No. 17 will form in First-street, down to East River.

The Committee in charge of the Car will place it on the West side of Second Avenue at Eighth-street.

Other Societies, not reported, will form on Second Avenue, with right on First street, with left down Christie-street, and, on their arrival, report to the D. G. Marshal, at 34 St. Mark's Place, near 2nd Av.

By order, HENRY STORMS,
Deputy Grand Marshal.

The Divisions will be arranged as follows: --

ORDER OF PROCESSION.

Mounted Escort.

The Grand Marshal, Thomas O'Conor, Esq., The Deputy Grand Marshal.

Aids.

FIRST DIVISION

Thomas M. Jenkins, Aid to Grand Marshal.
The Independent Sons of Erin, No. 1.
The Laborers' Union B. Society, 1st Section, No. 2.

SECOND DIVISION.

James Mulligan, Aid to Grand Marshal.
The L. Union Benevolent Society, 2nd Section,
William Foley, Marshal.

THIRD DIVISION.

Malachi Fallon, Aid to Grand Marshal.
The L. Union Benevolent Society, 3rd Section.
James Kilbride, Marshal.

FOURTH DIVISION.

Joseph F. Casserly, Aid to Grand Marshal.
The L. Union Benevolent Society, 4th Section,
P. Kohoe, Marshal.

FIFTH DIVISION.

Edward Shortill, Aid to Grand Marshal.
Hibernian Universal Benevolent Society, No. 3.
John Heany and Thomas Flynn, Marshals.
The Patterson Repealers & U. Sons of Erin, No. 4.
Henry J. Coddington, Marshal.
The E. Frat. Beneficial Society of Brooklyn, No. 5.

Joseph McMurray, Marshal.

The Mayors, and Common Councils of New-York, Brooklyn and Jersey City.

The Orator of the Day.
Invited Guests.
Officers of Foreign Vessels of War.
Officers of the Army and Navy.
Military generally.

SIXTH DIVISION

Major William Denman, Aid to Grand Marshal.

Mutes.

Pall Bearers. FUNERAL CAR. Pall Bearers.

Mutes.
Mourners.

The U. Irish Repeal Association of N. York, No. 6.
William Denman, Marshal.

SEVENTH DIVISION.

William McArdle, Aid to Grand Marshal.
The Hibernian Benevolent Burial Society, No. 7.
Dr. William O'Donnell, Marshal.
The Benevolent Society of Operative Masons, No. 8
William Furlong, Marshal.
The Emmet Mutual Benevolent Society, No. 9.
William Green, Marshal.
The Young Friends of Ireland, No. 10,
John P. Curran, Marshal.

EIGHTH DIVISION.

Captain Geissenhainer, Aid to Grand Marshal.
The R. C. Total Abstinence B. Society, No. 11.
John McGrath, Marshal.
The Shamrock B. Society of New-York, No. 12.
Hugh Finn, Marshal.
The U. Practical Stone Cutters of N. York, Brooklyn and Jersey City, No. 13.
William Young, Marshal.
The Friendly Sons of St. Patrick, No. 14.
The Irish Emigrant Society of New York, No. 15.
The Newark Hibernian Provident Society, No. 16.
The Newark Repeal Association

The Hibernian Prov. Society of New Haven, No. 17.

The Shamrock Benevolent Societies of New York and Brooklyn, united.

Citizens generally.

The line of march will be from Second Avenue, through Eighth-street to the Bowery, around Union Square, down Broadway to Grand-street, along Grand-street to the Bowery, through Chatham-street and Broadway to Fulton-street, through Fulton to Greenwich, to the Battery.

When the right reaches the Battery the portion of the line in front of the car will halt and form on the west side of Greenwich street. The car will then pass in front of the line, followed by the Officers, Orator, Guests, &c. to the Garden, and the line will then fall in and follow in order.

After the exercises in the Garden are terminated the column will be re-formed in the same order, and will proceed up Broadway, under the direction of the Grand Marshal.

A PLEA FOR ASSISTANCE IN EMIGRATING TO AMERICA, 1847

Source: "A Petition from the Poor Irish to the Right Honourable Lords Temporal and Spiritual," Appendix 25 to the Report of the Select Committee of the House of Lords on Colonization from Ireland, 1847.

"Honoured Gentlemen, We, the undersigned, humbly request that ye will excuse the liberty we are taking in troubling ye at a time when ye ought to be tired, listening to our cries of distress; but like beggars we are importunate. We, the undersigned, are the inhabitants of Rattibarren, Barony of Liny, County of Sligo. It is useless for us to be relating our distress, for ye too often were distressed by hearing them, -- for none could describe it; it can only be known by the sufferers themselves. We thank ye and our Gracious Sovereign, and the Almighty for the relief we have, though one pound of Indian meal for a full-grown person, which has neither milk nor any other kind of kitchen, it is hardly fit to keep life in them; but if we got all that we would be thankful. But if we have reason to complain, there is others has more reason to complain, for in the Parish Townagh they are getting but half a pound, and several of them are not able to buy one pennyworth of milk. I fear the curse of the Almighty will come heavier on this country, the way they are treating the poor, but distress stares us in the face more grim than ever, for we have no sign of employment, for the farmers is not keeping either boy or girl or workmen they can avoid, but are doing the work by their families, though they are not half doing it. In times past the poor of this country had large gardens of potatoes, and as much conacre as supported them for nearly the whole year, and when they had no employment from the farmers they were working for themselves, and when they had no employment they had their own provisions; but now there are thousands and tens of thousands that has not a cabbage plant in the ground; so we hope that ye will be so charitable as to send us to America, and give us land according to our families, and anything else ye will give us (and we will do with the coarsest kind). We will repay the same, with the interest thereof, by instalments, as the Government will direct. And if any refuse or neglect to pay the same, the next Settler to pay the money and have his land. And we will bind ourselves to defend the Queen's Right in any place we are sent, and leave it on our children to do the same. So we hoped for the sake of Him gave ye power and England power, and raised her to the wonder of the world, and enabled her to pay twenty millions for the slaves of India, that ye will lend us half the sum, which we will honestly repay, with the interest thereof, for we are more distressed than they; and hope for the sake of Him that said, 'He that giveth to the poor lendeth to the Lord, and He will repay it,' that ye will grant our petition. And may He grant ye heavenly wisdom, with temporal and spiritual riches also, is the earnest prayer of your petitioners."

Signed (eighty six names).

"We think it useless to ye with names, as we could get as many as would nearly reach across the Channel. We hope your Lordship will

will excuse the liberty we take in troubling you. We know that you have Irish poor at heart, and that you are their best friend, which is the cause of us making so free. We hope that ye will make allowance for deficiencies of this, for the writer is a poor man that knows little about stiles and titles, for we are not able to pay a man that could it right.

To Lord Monteagle, House of Lords, London.

CONDITIONS ON EMIGRANT SHIPS, 1847

Source: Minutes of Evidence before the Select Committee (Lords) on Colonization from Ireland (1847). pp. 45-48.

The fearful state of disease and debility in which the Irish emigrants have reached Canada must undoubtedly be attributed in a great degree to the destitution and consequent sickness prevailing in Ireland, but has been much aggravated by the neglect of cleanliness, ventilation and a generally good state of social economy during the passage, and has afterwards been increased and disseminated throughout the whole country in the mal-arrangements of the Government system of emigrant relief. Having myself submitted to the privations of a steerage passage in an emigrant ship for nearly two months, in order to make myself acquainted with the condition of the emigrant from the beginning, I can state from experience that the present regulations for ensuring health and comparative comfort to passengers are wholly insufficient, and that they are not and cannot be enforced, notwithstanding the great zeal and high abilities of the Government agents.

Before the emigrant has been a week at sea he is an altered man. How can it be otherwise? Hundreds of poor people, men, women and children of all ages, from the drivelling idiot of ninety to the babe just born, huddled together without light, without air, wallowing in filth and breathing a fetid atmosphere, sick in body, dispirited in heart, the fever patients lying between the sound, in sleeping places so narrow as almost to deny them the power of indulging, by a change of position, that natural restlessness of the disease; by their ravings disturbing those around, and predisposing them, through the effects of the imagination, to imbibe the contagion; living without food or medicine, except as administered by the hand of casual charity, dying without the voice of spiritual consolation, and buried in the deep without the rites of the Church. The food is generally ill-selected and seldom sufficiently cooked, in consequence of the supply of water, hardly enough for cooking and drinking, does not allow washing. In many ships the filthy beds, teeming with all abominations, are never required to be brought on deck and aired; the narrow space between the sleeping berths and the piles of boxes is never washed or scraped, but breathes us a damp and fetid stench, until the day before the arrival at quarantine, when all hands are required to 'scrub up', and put on a fair face for the doctor and Government inspector. No moral restraint is attempted, the voice of prayer is never heard; drunkenness, with its consequent train of ruffianly debasement, is not discouraged, because it is profitable to the captain, who traffics in the grog.

In this ship which brought me out from London last April, the passengers were found in provisions by the owners, according to a contract and a furnished scale of dietary.

"The meat was of the worst quality. The supply of water shipped on board was abundant, but the quantity served out to the passengers was so scanty that they were frequently obliged to throw overboard their salt provisions and rice (a most important article of their food) because they had not water enough both for the necessary cooking and the satisfying of their raging thirst afterwards.

They could only afford water for washing by withdrawing it from the cooking of their food. I have known persons to remain for days together in their dark, close berths because they thus suffered less from hunger, though compelled at the same time for want of water to heave overboard their salt provisions and rice.

No cleanliness was enforced, and the beds were never aired. The master during the whole voyage never entered the steerage, and would listen to no complaints; the dietary contracted for was, with some exceptions, nominally supplied, though at irregular periods; but false measures were used (in which the water and several articles of dry food were served), the gallon measure containing but three quarts, which fact I proved in Quebec and had the captain fined for. Once or twice a week ardent spirits were sold indiscriminately to the passengers, producing scenes of unchecked blackguardism beyond description; and lights were prohibited because the ship -- with her open fire-grates upon deck -- with lucifer matches and lighted pipes used secretely in the sleeping berths -- was freighted with Government powder for the garrison at Quebec.

The case of this ship was not one of peculiar misconduct; on the contrary, I have the strongest reason to know, from information I have received from very many emigrants well known to me, who came over this year in different vessels, that this ship was better regulated and more comfortable than many that reached Canada.

Disease and death among the emigrants, nay, the propagation of infection throughout Canada, are not the worst consequences of this atrocious system of neglect and ill-usage. A result far worse is to be found in the utter demoralisation of the passengers, both male and female, by the filth and debasement and disease of two or three months so passed. The emigrant, enfeebled in body and degraded in mind, even though he should have the physical power, has not the heart, has not the will to exert himself. He has lost his self-respect, his elasticity of spirit; he no longer stands erect; he throws himself listlessly upon the daily dole of Government, and in order to earn it carelessly lies for weeks on the contaminated straw of a fever lazaretto.

EDITORIAL TO THE EMIGRANTS OF 1849

Source: The Nation, New York, February 10, 1849.

My Friends - There may not be any use in addressing you this letter, since, though no people listen to advice more attentively, none are so sure to take their own way in the end. As a matter of duty, however, I write, and, for your own sake, I hope you will read.

Your common sense must be your guide in what you shall bring to America, and where you shall embark. But how you are to prepare yourselves for the new state of society into which you are going to be precipitated is what I am going to tell you. In very truth, you are bound for a new world, so new that you will feel "born again" on your landing.

You may buy in Cork, in Dublin, or in Liverpool, or wherever you sail from, a little shilling book, which I earnestly recommend to you as the best preliminary study for an Emigrant. It is called The Life of Franklin, and therein you will read how, by industry, system, and self-denial, a Boston printer's boy rose to be one of the most prosperous, honorable, and important citizens of the Republic. It will teach you that in America no beginning, however humble, can prevent a man from reaching any rank, however exalted; that, though the land does not grow gold, neither does it smother any energy by which fortune is created; that, above all, the genius of the people, and the State, is entirely and radically, practical. These are lessons you should have by heart.

This great, grizzly Continent needs an enormous increase of practical ability to clothe it with fullness and beauty. If you are coming with the idea that an easier living can be made here than elsewhere... turn back . . . . If you have learned Latin and Greek, I advise you, on your arrival, to keep it a profound secret, for otherwise you may utterly ruin your prospects. Not a word of your "classics," if you would not be written down as an ass. But if you can farm land, or work at a bench, or on a scaffold, or carry a hod, or mix mortar or medicine, or cast accounts, or unlade ships, come on fearlessly, and try your fortune. In short, if you are fit for any practical business in life, come forth and fear not.

While crossing the great sea and reading Franklin's Life, lose no opportunity of gaining information from your fellow travellers and exercising your powers of observation and reflection. You are coming into a land where knowledge is, absolutely, power. You, besides, are making a change which will test severely your moral principles. Cut adrift from all your early associations, you are about to fling yourself into a society where conscience, for a time, will be your sole observer. Meditate often on that great image of God over which you sail . . . Familiarize your mind with grave and solemn thoughts, which are the best preparatives for your new state of being. Think of Columbus, of Washington, and of all who have gone before you on that track, what their destiny has been, and what your own may be if you will it. Think always--reason on everything.

I would not have any in Ireland who can still keep their ground leave it now . . . . Let those who must come, come. But let them prepare for hard labor, and no patronage. No man here can make another man. Society throws the stranger almost on his own resources. But if he shows pluck and wit, every one wishes him well, and nobody stands in his way. If he has not the stamina of growth in him, he will fade and wither and fall like a badly transplanted tree, and, then, no more about him. Such is

America! Whosoever dare gallantly adventure into this new world, and trust to himself alone, will live to see the accuracy of this description, and to thank the voice that forewarned him of what he had really to encounter and expect.

As to the modes of crossing the Atlantic, there are various lines of packets. They all advertise in The Nation, and the companies are, no doubt, equally excellent. Only make the best bargain for the best ship, and you will come safely through. And don't forget to read Franklin by the way, and study his career, and how, from so lowly a beginning, he attained such an end. Take the moral of his life close to your hearts, and your success in America may yet, in a humble degree, resemble his. He made himself; so may you also.

Yours always,

T. D. McGee

THE IRISH-AMERICANS IN THE MEXICAN WAR, AS DESCRIBED BY GENERAL WINFIELD SCOTT, IN A LETTER TO THE JOURNALIST W. E. ROBINSON, JULY 2, 1850.

Source: Journal of the American Irish Historical Society, XXVI (1927), 256.

. . . In Mexico, we estimated the number of persons in the army, foreigners by birth, at about 3500, & of these more than 2000 were Irish. How many had been naturalized I can not say, but am persuaded that seven out of ten had at least declared their intentions, according to law, to become citizens . . . .

It is hazardous, or may be invidious, to make distinctions; but truth obliges me to say that, of our Irish soldiers--save a few who deserted from General Taylor, and had never taken the naturalization oath--not one ever turned his back upon the enemy or faltered in advancing to the charge. Most of the other foreigners, by birth, also behaved faithfully and gallantly.

EDWARD EVERETT HALE ON THE "CELTIC RACE" IN AMERICA, 1852.

Source: Boston Daily Advertiser, January 28, 1852.

Proportions of Original Races in America.

In writing these letters to the Boston Daily Advertiser, I attempted to confine myself to the facts which directly affect legislation or charitable action. There is, however, a curious question as to the effect to be produced on national character by intermixture of blood and race, produced by such large emigration as we see. What I have said in my last letter has been carefully guarded, so as to refer everywhere to the absolutely unmixed Celtic race. Of its value intermixed I have spoken as highly as I could.

An anxious question is asked, however, by men of the old American book, whether there is not an over-preponderance of the Celtic element coming in upon us? I do not profess to answer the question, how far the origin of the native American blood is Celtic.

In what proportions do the Celtic and Gothic or Germanic elements mingle in the Englishman of today (1852) and, of course, in the American of today? Dr. Kombst estimates in 1841 that there are of pure German blood in England 10,000,000.Of mixed blood where the Teutonic prevailed in England and the northeast of Ireland, 6,000,000. Of mixed blood, where the Celtic prevailed in England, Scotland and Ireland, 4,000,000. And of pure Celtic in Scotland, Wales and Ireland, 6,000,000.

But Dr. Lanthan, with more reason, I think, doubts the purity of any Germanic blood in England, saying that 'a vast amount of Celticism, not found in our tongue, very probably exists in our pedigrees.' And in another place he says that in nine-tenths of the displacements of races made by conquest the female half ancestry of the present inhabitants must have belonged to the beaten race.

I think the history of the Saxon invasions is such as to give color to this idea in the case of England. And I am not sure, but what it could be made out, that the American people, before the recent Irish invasion, showed in their proportion of black-haired men of dark complexion and other Celtic signs that as large a fraction as two-thirds of its blood ran in the dark ages of the past in Celtic veins. If this be so, if the proportion, two-thirds Celtic to one-third Gothic or Germanic is the proportion which makes up that 'perfect whole,' the 'true American,' which considers itself so much finer than either of the ingredients, the recent emigrations furnish a happy co-incidence with the original law. For five past years the arrivals at New York, which are three-fourths the whole, and represent it in kind exactly, have been 547,173 Irish; 278,458 Germanic; 153,969 English and Scotch; 71,359 others. Now keep these 71,359 'others' for condiments in the mixture. There are Norwegians and French, Belgians and Spaniards, Swiss and Italians, balanced against each other (and a few Magyars).

The English, of course, we need not count; but of pure Celts and pure Germans we have to fraction just two to one; and in that proportion are they to affect the blood of the American people.

This computation which I had prepared before I read a courteous article in the American Celt of January 24, 1852, will, perhaps, show to the writer of that paper, that we are not so far apart in our views as he supposed.

IRISH-AMERICAN SCHOOLCHILDREN IN BOSTON, 1855.

Source: Letter from J. H. Philbrick, Superintendent of Schools, Boston, to the Editor of the Boston Transcript, August 1, 1855.

James Anthony Froude, in his recent rapid passage across the country on the homeward stretch of his round-the-world trip, was interviewed in New York and among other things was asked for reminiscences of his visit to the United States.

The reading of his interview revived the memory of an incident of the visit, which is perhaps worth relating.

During this visit, Mr. Froude delivered lectures in the principal cities on the Irish question. The theory which he propounded and advocated was, that the troubles in Ireland were not the result of bad government at all, but of bad blood in the Irish race. But he was anxious to get more light on the subject, if possible, and so, when in Boston, he wanted to visit public schools which were frequented by children of the Irish race. Accordingly, I took him to some boys' schools and some girls', where the children were almost wholly of Irish parentage. At the last of these girls' schools, of the grammar grade installed in a splended new school house of large size, after passing through twelve or fourteen rooms, filled with bright, well-dressed girls full of animation in their recitation in the various branches of instruction, Mr. Froude asked: "Do you mean to say that these are the children of Irish immigrants?" "Yes," I answered, "I believe there is not a single pupil in this school of the Yankee race." "Well," he continued," I must confess I'm staggered." "Now," said I, "I will take you to a mixed school (boys and girls being in separate rooms and classes), which stands on a spot that two years ago was a mud hole in a marsh surrounded by poor dwellings, mostly occupied by Irish immigrants."

After passing through most of the rooms in the fine building, in which were neatly-dressed pupils in the most perfect order, earnestly engaged in their work, we came to a boys' room where a recitation in history was in progress. Here he took a seat and proceeded to question the class, from which he got very prompt and appropriate answers. At length, he singled out a little tan-headed boy of the Irish nationality and plied him with a lot of pretty hard questions, but every one was answered with admirable promptness and accuracy. Mr. Froude stopped, remained silent for a short time with his eyes cast down as though in a profound study. He then addressed the boys again and said: "My boys, where did you learn this?" "Out of a book, sir," was the ready reply. "And where did you get the book?" "Out of the public library," was the answer.

Mr. Froude then arose to leave and I said: "Now, Mr. Froude, I will take you to the Girls' High School, where you will find representatives of the Irish nationality in a higher grade of instruction." "Well," replied Mr. Froude, "you may take me where you please; it makes no difference; I'm full; I can't hold any more."

SOME ADVICE TO THE IRISH EMIGRANT

Source: Editorial in The Irish News, June 20, 1857.

To gain a foothold on this free soil is the first duty of the Irish exile. As the land is the true basis and source of national greatness, so its possession gives to individuals happiness and independence . . . . But the Irish in Ireland, asking our advice, will inquire first, "Should we emigrate?" If so, "is royal Canada better for us than the Republic?" We repeat our former opinion, that every Irishman who enjoys anything like comfort at home should stay at home . . . . Let the Irish farmers and merchants stay in Ireland. If they fight for themselves only half as well, and work for themselves only half as well as Irishmen must do here, they will soon be a free and happy nation.

But to all the Irish laborers and operatives who live from hand to mouth, competing against each other for bare animal subsistence -- to the . . . masses of Victoria's subjects who cannot possibly raise themselves above the verge of starvation, we say, come out, if you should beg your passage money. Thus only can you raise the value of labor in the home market, thus only can you benefit yourselves and the laborers you leave behind. As long as you crowd each other, political economy and Acts of Parliament are omnipotent to make you as you are -- chattel property, surplus labor, a drug on the market, cheaper and more pitiable than negro slaves.

The laboring men of Europe are placed in that dilemma that they must either revolutionize or migrate. We believe that extensive emigrations precede revolutions. The working men, relieved of the great press of competition and feeling more power and independence will revolutionize, and by crushing hereditary monopolies, open up the resources of their country . . . . Let emigration be vigorously pushed. It is the sword that cuts the gordian knot of political economy, legislative sophistry, and oppression.

But if emigrants crowd each other and cause labor to stagnate in our seaports, they only transplant their difficulties to this side of the ocean. We say, then, push out Westward. There is your home, and the manifest destiny that God has provided for you.

Before entering on the comparison between royal Canada and the Republic, it may be asked, how are Irish Emigrants to proceed? Are they to segregate themselves and go en masse like the Mormons or Germans? This mode, even if desirable, is not practicable for the Irish. It might have been done with advantage some years ago, but not now. Because there is neither the machinery nor the desire among the Irish at home to organize themselves. The Germans are organized because they have a government of some kind. In Ireland there is no government -- nothing but a rent, tax, and tithe-gathering garrison. The Catholic clergy now, more than ever, desire to keep the Irish in Ireland. They do not, and will not, organize wholesale emigration. Therefore, Irishmen push out boldly and individually. It is true, most of them expect to meet friends here, who have, perhaps, helped them. Yet, altogether, they are the most self-reliant body that has arrived on our shores.

This self-reliance, that broke the dearest hometies, should not be destroyed by mock patronage. We don't say that all the Irish, on landing here, should be left to their self-reliance. That they have been neglected by the wealthy and intelligent Irish at home, who should have guided their exiled steps is no reason why we should abandon them . . . We should have temporary homes for the poor or sick immigrants. Above all, there should be an Intelligence Office, to supply information regarding the quality and price of land, the climate, topography, water resources, mineral state of the surrounding country, population, wages, means of conveyance, etc., in all parts of the continent. The great danger of such an office is that speculators might use it for selfish purposes. However, the evil might be avoided. We might go thus far without destroying the Irishman's self-reliance. But the scheme proposed, sometime ago, by the Buffalo Convention would only patronize the immigrant, without affording substantial aid commensurate with the risks to be met in the unknown terrors of the swamp, the prairies, or the bush. The Convention, while proposing to aid the immigrant, could only push his self-reliance beyond rational limit. Every poor immigrant is not a hardy pioneer, like the celebrated Irishman Davy Crockett, the type of the backwoodsman.

Experience has given melancholy proof that the great majority of squatters, raised in the cultivated lands of Europe, find themselves mere children in the presence of unredeemed nature. For want of skill, such persons are sure to expend ten times the labor necessary in felling trees, chopping them up, clearing away underbrush, draining, etc. He overworks himself, gets the ague, and generally has to abandon his advanced position, hire himself to a farmer for a living, and learn something of the ways of the country. Then, he may go out and squat, keeping within hail of his neighbor. This is what he should do at first; work his way gradually. This is the only path to healthful, steady, and successful colonization. There are some iron sinewed Celts who can live and thrive anywhere; but we speak for the crowd of our poor, earnest, but inexperienced countrymen. Early colonization progressed in this way, without patronage of any kind, or in spite of corporation patronage, which is generally an incubus.

Our people might be organized at home if they had a government, or a true national spirit. But the Irish in America are peculiarly unadapted for being herded or led, in anything but military companies. Strangers to each other, often bitterly oppossed in mere questions of leadership, impatient under injustice or humbug at home their docility is not increased in a country where they expect full freedom; sharpened by misfortune and perhaps over-watchful against imposture, the Irish are notoriously irascible and quarrelsome among themselves. They do not pull harmoniously together in society like the Scotch and Germans.

The Irish agree better with strangers than with each other. In short, excepting their family affection, they are Americans before they land. United as no other people are in general principles, but personally independent, their only alternative is to go ahead in true American fashion; every man on his own hook; not slapdash into the prairie, swamp, or forest, as recommended by some, but steadily and cautiously, as we have indicated.

The number of Irish who have left our Eastern cities and gone Westward this spring is unprecedented. These thousands go independently, with out the aid of conventions. The only danger is that there will be a stampede. Year by year, as the pioneers advance they will draw their friends after them . . . .

If the Irish man had no alternative but landlord oppression at home or transportation to the American Siberia [Canada] , with its comparative liberty, we would hesitate to advise him to emigrate. But when the choice is between Canada and the United States, we recommend the latter without prejudice. No one but a mendacious and interested agent of Royalty would dare to say that the material advantages of Canada equal those of the Western States.

THE "FIGHTING 69TH" AND ITS COLONEL, 1861.

Source: The Irish American (New York), October 26, 1861.

To the Editor of the Irish American:

Sir -- As anything relating to the late campaign of the 69th, and the present unfortunate position of its brave Colonel and some of its members, must be interesting to your readers. I desire to lay before them through the medium of your wide spread columns, the following sketch as well to correct certain prevalent erroneous impressions as to present some facts on the subject hitherto unpublished, and unknown to the public.

Popular as the corps was it had many grievances (most of which were owing to the hastiness of its organization, and the shortness of its term of service) but it seems to me that the report of Brigadier General Sherman after the Battle of Bull Run, contains a statement which does the greatest injustice to the regiment, and which has become the heavier grievance from being borne in silence and thereby tacitly admitted. He says, 'After the repulse of the 2nd Wisconsin regiment the ground was open for the 69th, who advanced and held it for some time, but finally fell back in confusion.' He omitted saying what many witnessed, and what Colonel Corcoran confirmed in Richmond (when he first saw the report) that he rode up and ordered Col. Corcoran to draw off his men, while we were still obstinately maintaining our ground, not only against the main strength of the Confederates already engaged, but also while pressed hard on the right flank by the fresh troops (Johnson's) which General Smith and Col. Elzey had just brought from Manassas, and which according to the official report of those officers, numbered 8,000 men. I do not pretend to say that we could have held to position against such overwhelming odds, but as we did so until ordered to abandon it, simple justice and fair play should have prompted Sherman to tell the whole truth. The manner in which he managed or mismanaged his brigade is more open to comment than the conduct of any regiment during the day. Inferior in numbers as we were to the enemy, he increased the disadvantage by keeping one excellent corps idle (the 13 N. Y. V.) and bringing the others into action separately and successively, allowing one to be broken before another was brought to its support, and thus throwing away the only chance of success that remained. Not withstanding the heavy reinforcements the Confederates had received they were so badly beaten and disheartened up to this time that there can scarcely be a doubt but that a vigorous simultaneous and combined attack of Sherman's Brigade and Keyes would have carried their position. Instead of this, after our regiment (leading the column) had turned their right under Gen. Evans, dispersed and almost destroyed the crack corps of the South -- the N. O. Zouaves, instead of following up our advantage and pushing home the flying foe we gave them time to change their position, concentrate their strength, and deploy their fresh troops. We have reason to be thankful that our ill timed delay was not entirely fatal to us, as it would have been, had not Beauregard's order to General Ewall to get in our rear miscarried.

Again, when our attack failed and the retreat began, Col. Corcoran endeavoured to cover it by forming the men in squares, in which order it moved to the point at which we crossed Bull Run, where on account of the woods and the narrowness of the path down the bluffs that formed the west bank, it had to be reduced to a column. Sherman, who was in the Square, told the men to get away as fast as they could as the enemy's cavalry were coming. This prevented Col. Corcoran from reforming the men in square on the other side of the Run, a movement which would have not only effectually repelled the enemy, but also have covered the retreat of every battery lost subsequently. It was in his endeavors to remedy the disorder and straggling caused by this 'license to run' that Colonel Corcoran (who from the unfortunate and irreparable loss of Haggerty, and the absence of all his staff was obliged to be somewhat in the rear) was cut off from the main body of the regiment, by the enemy horse, and being able to rally only nine men, moved into a small house to make a better defense, but was induced by some of his officers to surrender as resistance was hopeless. Meantime about half a dozen men had joined him at the house, of whose arrival he was ignorant. Trifling as the reinforcement was he surrendered without a desperate fight. I shared his subsequent misfortunes, and witnessed the manly fortitude with which he bore them, and the consistent dignity which repelled all overtures for any parole that would tie up his hands from the Union cause and repulsed some Southern friends who endeavoured to induce him from it.

It may not be improper to sketch his prison life. Owing to the inadequate arrangements for our accommodation in Richmond it was the afternoon of the 4th before some of us got anything to eat, so that we had eaten only once in four days. The Colonel was extremely exhausted but desired that all his men to be brought to him 'that he might take a look at and know' as he said, 'those who had done their duty to the last.' Learning that some had no money and wanted clothing badly, he gave $20.00 of his own scanty resources to be laid out for their use. He was never allowed to go, even to the hospital, to see his wounded men, which later I heard him complain somewhat of. He was kept quite apart from us who were in the same building, although some of us managed to see him daily or oftener. I wish to contradict, however, a statement which has obtained universal currency about him and which is an unmitigated falsehood. He never was in irons nor was he threatened with them from his capture until he was removed to Charleston on the 10th ult. When we saw him, rigidly as he was watched, and great as was the importance attached to his safekeeping -- the consistent bearing of which I have already spoken, had won for him the respect of every Southerner, and though it at first, drew on him the virulent abuse of the Richmond press, even it ultimately changed its tone and declared 'that the consistent obstinacy of that most imprudent and inveterate of the Yankee prisoners Col. Corcoran was preferable by far to the repentent professions and cringing of some prisoners to obtain a parole.' As to our general treatment it was harsh, although as long as any hope of the government making an exchange remained, our guards were courteous and communicative, and I feel bound to say that the cavalry to whom we surrendered (Clay Dragoons) acted in every respect like chivalrous and honourable men. Lately, however, some regiments -- mere conscript boys, whom the ten percent levy had drawn out, committed great atrocities on the prisoners, firing through the windows at us on the slightest pretence of breach of the regulations. Several shots were fired into the room where the 69th were confined, and one man of the 2nd. N. Y. S. M., was wounded in the arm. Shots fired into the buildings were said to have resulted fatally, but as we could not get to them I cannot vouch for the fact positively. Atrocities like these coupled with the prospect of being sent further south, induced many to try and escape, but the great majority failed, and were put in irons. As, however, none of the 69th, save two who were unsuccessful, had tried, your correspondent thought it became the honor of the corps to make an attempt, and accompanied by Sergeant O'Donohue, of Co. K. and Peter Kelly of Co. J., left Richmond on the 18th. ult. passing the sentries in disguise. Capt. McIvor who intended to accompany us was unfortunately suspected by the new guard, and put in irons. I regret to see he has since been sent to New Orleans. Our provisions (21 lbs. of crackers) soon ran out, but Virginia is full of corn, and we lived on the enemy. After traveling a week (solely at dead of night) we came on the Confederate lines on the Potomac, above Aquia Creek and after running into the most advanced cavalry outpost, from which we escaped narrowly, and coming in contact with sentries for miles along the river we at length found shelter and concealment in a deserted fishing house. Having built a raft to reach the Potomac fleet which was in sight, it turned out to be too small, and O'Donohue embarked alone on it and reached the Seminole, the captain of which, however, refused to send a boat for us who remained on the Virginia shore, and insisting on sending O'Donohue to Washington. We were left to our own resources, and built another raft on which we reached the Penguin during the following night, and were sent aboard the Yankee. The engineer Mr. Carpenter, and one of the crew furnished me with a complete suit of clothing which took away my naked half savage appearance, and the steward Mr. Fitzpatrick attended to our famished and ravenous appetites with similar humanity. As this aid was in no way official, and came solely from the generous and humane spirit we shall always cherish grateful feelings towards these gentlemen. From Lieutenant Ross, of the Navy Yard, Washington and the captain of the Philadelphia steamer, we received similar kind treatment. Trusting that the length of this communication will not render it objectionable.

I am, Sir, Yours truly,
James M. Rorty.

IRISH-AMERICANS AND THE DRAFT RIOTS IN NEW YORK, 1863.

Source: New York Post, July 17, 1863.

Archbishop Hughes has called a meeting of what he styles "the men of New York who are now called in many of the papers rioters." They are to meet near his house at two o'clock to-day. We have satisfied ourselves that the call is genuine, and that the Archbishop means to speak to the rioters, though he declined to give to the reporter, sent from this office to see him, any idea of the nature of the address he proposes to make to these persons.

We hope none others than the rioters will attend the meeting. The call is addressed to these alone; the advice they will receive can be read by peaceable and honest citizens in the journals, and it is highly desirable that in the present state of the city no crowd should collect anywhere.

We think it especially desirable that those Irish citizens who have taken no part in these riots shall stay away from this meeting. The character of the Irish has suffered greatly in the public esteem in the last few days. There is already a disposition -- unjust, but not unnatural under the circumstances -- to confound and condemn in a body all people of Irish birth or parentage. This is wrong. We know of many instances in which Irishmen have been warm and efficient supporters of the law. In the First Ward of this city the Irish porters and laborers have been formed into a guarding force, and have dispersed incipient riots, arrested a countryman of their own who was attempting to create a disturbance, and rescued one poor negro from the clutches of a mob. We are assured that there are other similar instances. It is highly important that the public should be enabled to distinguish between these two classes -- the riotous, and the orderly and industrious. The meeting called by the Archbishop affords an excellent occasion for drawing the line; and we hope to see the peaceable and industrious Irish availing themselves of it. Their shepherd has summoned the wolves; let not the sheep attend also; let them stay at home, mind their usual business, and leave the wolves to be dealt with.

In the meantime the Archbishop's call, if it is generally obeyed, will draw together a crowd of such miscreants, assassins, robbers, house burners and thieves, such a congregation of vicious and abandoned wretches, as is not often got together. The police should be on the lookout there; they may catch many an incendiary, many a murderer, many a highway robber; and we cannot conceive that the Archbishop's safeguard could extend or that he would lend his protection to such malefactors.

Of course a strong force of the military, both cavalry and artillery, will be stationed near by, ready to act promptly and with the utmost vigor. This experiment of raising the devil is a new one. It is not easy to tell what he will do when he is raised.

ARCHBISHOP HUGHES AND THE DRAFT RIOTS, 1863.

Source: New York Herald, July 18, 1863.

Men of New York: They call you rioters, but I cannot see a rioter's face among you (applause). I call you man of New York, not gentlemen, because gentlemen is so threadbare a term that it means nothing positive (applause). Give me men, and I know of my own knowledge that if the city were invaded by British or any other foreign power you would prove yourselves so (great applause). The delicate ladies of New York with their infants at their breasts would look for their protection to men more than to gentlemen (applause). Of course all this is no reason why you should not be gentlemen also, because there is no contradiction between the two. I address you to-day by my own voice -- no one has prompted me. If I could have met you anywhere I should have gone, even though on crutches (great applause, and cries of "God bless you"). But I could not say my limbs are weaker than my lungs. But it does gratify me to see you. You have met me in such quiet and good order -- though that does not surprise me, for it is what I should have expected. I do not address you as the President, or the Governor (laughter and applause), or the Mayor (renewed laughter), or military commander. No; I address you as your Father. (A voice -- "A commander above the whole of them.")

I am not going to treat of the question that has brought about this unhappy excitement; it is not my business. For myself, you know that I am a minister of God, a minister of peace, a minister who in your own trials in years past, you know, never deserted you. (Great applause, and cries of "Never, never.") With my tongue and with my pen I have stood by your fortunes always, and so shall I to the end, as long as you are right and I hope you are not wrong. I am not a runaway bishop in times of danger. It has been, perhaps, a calamity, but I do not regret it, that I never was conscious of fear until the danger was over, and then sometimes I became nervous (laughter and applause). I could not, because the laws of God forbid it. I could not fight for you in a just cause, but I could stand by you, advise you, and die with you (great applause).

Now, I have said that I should not enter into the question of grievances that have created this unhappy excitement in New York. I have no doubt that there are some real, I am convinced that there are many imaginary, causes. In this world everything is comparative; and I know no people on the face of the earth that have not their grievances, and I know no people on the face of the earth that have not greater grievances than we can complain of after all. Everything is comparative, and change does not always imply an improvement. There is a great difference! and when I think of its oppression, when I see the fertile West and South of Ireland depopulated and cattle browsing on the ruins of the cottages of the people that once lived there, I thank God that I am among friends and had an opportunity to come to a country where at least no such wretched tyranny is practised (great applause). If you are Irishmen, as your enemies say that the rioters are, I am an Irishman, too (applause), and I am not a rioter (laughter and applause). No, I am a man of peace. (A voice -- "So are we." "I hope so," the Archbishop replied.) If you are Catholics, as they have reported, probably to wound my feelings, then I am a Catholic, too (renewed applause). I know perfectly well that, except under misguidance or misconception, imaginary grievances, though we, or at least myself, cannot fathom them down to their rights and radical features, assume fearful proportions. I am aware that people will get uneasy sometimes, and yet I do think that every man, even myself as Bishop of the Church, for I have had my troubles and persecutions, should think with the poet that it is better to bear patiently, and especially because they are temporary and will pass away with slight inconveniences, the ills that we may be subject to, rather than rush upon evils that we have not yet known.

In Europe, where most of the countries are despotic, -- and even though they call themselves constitutional, as in England, they are not a bit the less despotic on the account, -- but in those countries where the ruler of right, whether he be a fool or a wise man, must occupy the throne there is no relief for an oppressed populace except a revolution. Now, revolution is a desperate resource in any country; and I have known no country to come out of it better than it was before it entered it. But in this country it is not the same kind of revolution. In this country the Constitution has made it the right of the people to make a revolution quietly every four years. Is not that so? (Laughter and applause.) Well, their battles in these revolutions are not of bloodshed and violence, and you know what they are fought with -- ballots, not bullets. Were you ever in Rome? If you have been there during the carnival you have seen the people go up and down the Corso in open carriages in a perpetual current, and they pelt each other with sugar-plums and bullets of flour. That is the way we must make revolutions. The Constitution of the government -- I do not now speak of the Governors, but the government - is a base and foundation which must not be disturbed (applause). It is the right of the people every four years to approve or disapprove, to correct or amend, as the printers say, the superstructure -- any one part of the superstructure that is absolutely necessary. But let them preserve the foundation, and let the American people in their wisdom build their own superstructure at least every four years. But, take away the foundations, and what shall you, or what shall I have to cling to in the form of human government? I am too old now to seek another home or another country. I want to cling by the old foundations of this, and I want the men who shall constitute the architects of the superstructure to be the right kind of men. But I have no opinion to express on that point. I am not a legislator. Everything is in the hands of the supreme people of the United States, and the majority of them, whether they make a blunder or not, must govern us; and I am willing to be governed by the majority (great applause). Now, gentlemen -- I beg your pardon, I mean men -- I am nearly done, but there is one thing more, there is a question which I wish to ask you, and I wish you to answer. I wish to ask your counsel. You will give it to me on another point, but in the meantime, are you willing that I should give you, as the Archbishop of New York, a word of advice? (Voices -- "Yes, yes.") I have not scolded you. I hope you would not deserve it, and I conclude just now as I began, with the observation that I have not seen in this vast audience a single countenance that I could set down as the countenance of a rioter. Then is this business to go on? Are we to be kept in terror? Is not every man, for his own sake, as well as for the sake of his neighbors, and of the city, to become in his own modest way a preserver of order and peace? (Applause.) Now I am told, and I have seen in the papers, that not a little property has been destroyed; I do not say by you; I hope not -- but I remember an anecdote of a lady who had a little boy about seven years of age, and she said to him, "Come, my darling, it is time to get ready to go to church." "Well," the child answered, "Well, ma, I'm willing to go wherever you go, but as to going to church, what's the use?" -- Well, that was the expression of a child -- I hope he has learned better since; but if property is destroyed, I say, "What's the use?" It must be paid for, by you and by me, and by everybody. "What's the use?" No, no, let us be careful of that. But if property be destroyed it can be replaced; but if lives are lost, the departed souls cannot be recalled from the other world. And although in case of an unjust and violent assault upon your rights without provocation (cheers), my notion is, that a man has a right to defend his shanty, if it be no more (cheers), or his house (cheers), or his church (cheers), at the risk of his life; but the cause must be always just; it must be defensive, not aggressive.

By the by, if you permitted me to give an advice, well, do you know what my advice would be? I will express it perfectly. It would be strange if I did not suffer much in my feelings by these reports, but these calumnies, as I hope they are, against you and against me, that you are rioters, and this and that. You cannot imagine that I could see and hear such things without feeling deeply. Is there no way in which directly or indirectly you can put a stop to these proceedings? At least let such of you as love God and revere the laws of the country, of which not a single statute has been enacted against you either as Irish or as Catholics, withdraw from crowds; because you have as well as others, suffered enough already; because no government can stand, can protect itself, unless it shall be able to protect its people (applause); because if you do not, the military force will be let loose upon you, and you know what that means: the innocent shall be shot down, and if there be guilty, they are the ones most likely to escape. As to advice, would it not be better for you, like me, to retire calmly and quietly to your homes? Not to give up your principles and convictions (applause), but keep out of the crowd in which immortal souls are launched into eternity without a moment's notice. Would not that be good advice? ("Yes, yes.")

And now there is another thing on which I would ask your advice and counsel, and it is this, namely: that if, when the smoke clears away, the responsibility of these so-called riots shall be thrown upon Catholics, especially Irish Catholics, and centred upon my heart, I wish you would tell me in what country I should claim to have been born (voices, "Ireland"). Yes, but what do you say if these stories are true? What do you say? Ireland! that never committed by her own sons, or on her own soil, until she was oppressed, a single act of cruelty. Ireland, that has been the mother of heroes and poets, but never the mother of a coward (applause) Perhaps you will think that this is Blarney (laughter); no, no, it is a fact. (A voice -- "History tells it.")

When the first Apostle of Christianity went to Ireland his name was not Patrick; he had been preceded by Pelagius -- he went there, and his course prepared the way. But when St. Patrick came he spoke to the multitude, and they listened to him; to the doctrines of Christianity, just as you have been patient enough to listen to me to-day. Look here, men; the soil of Ireland was never crimsoned or moistened by a single drop of martyr's blood, and that is what no other nation can say. In fact, it touches me deeply to have to revert to that country. I now so many noble things that are characteristic of the Irish. I know that Ireland is not a country that produces fools. Sometimes there are idiots, a few, and yet even they have all a spark of Irish wit; and the delicacy of feeling is so nice that they never say the word idiot, but they call a person of that description an "innocent"; because by their religious training they know the difference between moral right and wrong, and when the poor boy or girl is in that way they do not know the difference, and therefore the delicacy, which not even French can equal, calls them "innocents." There was once one of these "innocents," no longer a boy, who was very fond of eating raw eggs, and sometimes they were not quite as fresh as they might be. It appears that once when he was swallowing his favorite beverage a little chicken began to cry out of his throat, and he said: I am sorry for it, but you spoke too late." But there are few of that stamp in Ireland. That is a soil for other fruit than this.

Even when those protections generally employed for the good of the country which gave them birth were cut off, what scenes rise before my memory just now, when I think of the noble men that have been exiled under circumstances more trying than those which you and I have had to experience! -- the O'Donnells of Spain, who were at the head of that nation; Field Marshal Nugent, whom I knew intimately; the O'Donnell who saved the life of the young Emperor by interposing his own body between his sovereign and the assassin -- when I know that most of the universities on the continent of Europe were founded and established by the sons of Ireland (applause); when I know that in later times of persecution the blood of their brethren has fattened the fields of Balaklava and the Crimea; that they have strewn the plains round Delhi in India; when I think of the cruelty that has so treated them, leaving them no door open to a fair chance without any favor, except the United States; when I think of all this, be sure of it that I do not envy the policy of John Bull (great applause) in replacing a noble population by a set of fat bullocks (great applause). Now, men, I took upon myself to say that you should not be molested in paying me a visit or in returning from the visit, and you have not been. I thank you for your kindness, and I hope that nothing shall occur until you go to your homes at least; and if you by chance should see a policeman or military man, just look at him.

RESOLUTION PASSED BY FENIAN CONGRESS AT CHICAGO NOVEMBER, 1863.

Source: Report of the Proceedings . . . of the Special Commission . . . for the Trial of Thomas Clarke Luby, Dublin, 1866, 219-20.

Whereas, it has been proved to the Fenian Brotherhood, not alone through the authorized reports of the Head Centre, but also through the forced acknowledgements conveyed in certain recent denunciations emanating from the enemies of the Irish race, that there exists among the men of Ireland a numerous and widely extended national organization, which was heretofore named The Irish Revolutionary Brotherhood, but which, having grown in numbers and power, in subordination to its constituent authorities, and in discipline under the wise and able directions of its central executive, is now known as the Irish Republic, be it resolved --

That we, the centres and delegates of the Fenian Brotherhood, assembled in this convention, do hereby proclaim the Republic of Ireland to be virtually established, and moreover that we pledge ourselves to use all in our influence, and every legitimate privilege within our reach, to promote the full acknowledgement of its independence by every free government in the world.

AN ATTEMPT TO DIVERT THE "IRISH VOTE," 1867.

Source: Editorial in the New York Tribune, November 26, 1867.

The nomination of Fernando Wood and Mr. Hoffman, neither of whom has a drop of Irish blood in his veins, for Mayor of a city, three-fourths of whose Democratic voters are Irish, is an insult to the honor of the Old Sod, which every true Irish Democrat will avenge if he is not lost to all sense of the glory of the land that bore him. Is there never an Irish Democrat in New York fit to be elected Mayor after their long service in the ranks of the party? Must the Connollys, Sweeneys, McCluskeys, O'Briens and Raffertys, and Lynches and Shaughnessys, and McCarnochons, and O' Mahoneys, and the rest of the Irish race, all stand aside for these American hucksters in Irish votes? Have not the Irishmen of New York been excluded from the offices long enough? Awake, slumbering sons of old Ireland, and give such a demonstration of your affection for the Irish name and blood as will command the reverence of those miscreants, who are introducing each other to the Irish vote, as the Scotch lawyer introduced to his crony a client whom he could not serve, being retained on the other side. "Here," he wrote, "are two fat geese; pluck you the ane, and I'll the ither." The Irish vote in New York is enough to elect two Mayors. Wood and Hoffman agree to pluck it between them. But where is the Irish candidate? Why not elect an Irish Mayor, on an exclusively Irish ticket, with a shillilah and a short rope, without benefit of clergy, for the American that ventures to offer to vote for it? Irishmen stand up for your rights and the Mayoralty is yours. How do you know that Fernando will not turn around, enforce the liquor laws, as he did before, come "Reform" dodge, and bother you all like the mischief? How do you know but that Hoffman may sell you out to the Temperance people for their votes in the rural districts for Governor? Don't trust the tricky dogs. Nominate an Irishman, elect an Irishman, and then, when you call upon him in the City Hall, you've got an Irish Mayor as sure as there's never a snake nor a toad in Ireland.

EDITORIAL IN THE IRISH CITIZEN, NEW YORK, JUNE 12, 1869.

THE "IRISH VOTE"

There can be no doubt that the vote of at least half a million Irish-born citizens would be at the service of the party . . . which should really and bona fide press on and bring to pass a war against England. And Irish citizens, as citizens of the United States, would be quite well justified in so disposing of their votes as to bring about that most just and needful war; because it would be a strength and a blessing to their adopted country. It would operate as the best and promptest reconstruction, or rather, reconciliation, of the South. It would leave the United States in full possession of all their own continent. It would give profitable employment to hundreds of thousands of men who are now idle. It would carry off a vast mass of the floating and loafing population of our cities. It would abolish the monopoly of British shipowners, a monopoly secured to them during our war by the ravages of the Confederate cruisers. It would destroy the cordon of English maritime fortresses which affront and threaten our shores, from Halifax all the way round, by the Bermudas and Bahamas, to Jamaica. Lastly, such a war would settle our financial difficulties, in the only way they ever will be settled, namely, by repudiation.

We do not say, that by breaking up the British empire, it would also free Ireland, because this is not the point. It is with reference to America, and in our capacity as American citizens (as if there were no Ireland in the world) that we would give our heartiest support to that party in the United States which bases itself on war with England. But what party does so? Let there be no humbug; no party, no statesman of any party having the slightest pretension to give a direction to our foreign policy, has the slightest intention or idea of bringing on that war. Sumner, whose famous speech in the Senate has at least disgruntled the English, is perhaps the one man in America most hostile to the Irish, most thoroughly servile to England. His speech was not intended to bring on war, has no tendency whatsoever to a warlike policy; but his party, which is the predominant one now, has no objection to use the Irish national feeling in this country as a kind of threat to England . . . . It is easy for Yankee politicians to give us cheap talk of this sort; but any Irishman who gives his vote or his support to the Radical party, or any other party, with the idea that he is thereby promoting a war against the enemy of his native country, will be . . . much deluded . . . .

On the whole, it would be safer and wiser for the Irish adopted citizens of this Republic to abandon altogether the idea of the "Irish vote." It does no good, either to the country they have left, or to the one they have found. It exposes them to be cheated by lying politicians and to be sold and delivered by intriguing contractors for votes. They should exercise their privileges as American citizens, according to their best judgment of the interests and honor of their adopted country.

In the meantime, let them be assured that there will be no war with England.

AN APPEAL TO IRISH-AMERICAN VOTERS, 1872.

Source: Editorial in The Irish World, October 5, 1872.

Twenty-five Reasons Why Horace Greeley Ought to be Elected:

1. Because he is emphatically a man of the people.
2. Because he is opposed by Harper's Weekly.
3. Because "the interests of England demand that he should be defeated."
4. Because his defeat would give a renewed lease of power to a corrupt and dangerous party.
5. Because he had been the steadfast enemy of slavery, proscription and bigotry.
6. Because he will aid in colonizing the great West with the surplus population of our large cities.
7. Because his policy of reconciliation is founded on a humane principle and will dissipate the memory of a past hate.
8. Because he has sympathized with and aided suffering Ireland.
9. Because by word and example he has taught the true dignity of labor.
10. Because we want a man of ideas at the helm -- not a know-nothing.
11. Because his earnest efforts will be devoted to ameliorate the condition of the workingman.
12. Because his "Homestead Law" has made millions of men happy and prosperous.
13. Because he believes that the public land should be given to the people, not to railroad corporations.
14. Because he is opposed to "rings", civil and military.
15. Because he has aided in every good reform.
16. Because he will not squander the people's money.
17. Because he will uphold the simple dignity which becomes the chief magistrate of a republic.
18. Because he is no toady or Prince worshipper.
19. Because he will select for his Cabinet men of recognized ability and probity without reference to race, creed or color.
20. Because he opposed Know-Nothingism.
21. Because his election will defeat the English party.
22. Because he will restore the Union and States Rights, the foundations of the Constitution.
23. Because he believes in more rational employment than cock-fighting, horse-racing and bullpup training.
24. Because he will reform and elevate the sphere of politics.
25. Because he is supported by the ablest and honestest men and journals in the country.

Twenty-five Reasons Why Grant Should Not be Re-elected:

1. Because he is the candidate of Harper's Weekly.
2. Because he is on the same ticket with Wilson, the unrepentant Know-Nothing.
3. Because he is supported by all the proscriptive sectarians in the country.
4. Because, according to the London Echo, "the interests of England demand his re-election."
5. Because he is ignorant of the first principles of statesmanship.
6. Because his personal habits disqualify him.
7. Because he is at Long Branch when he should be in Washington.
8. Because he has usurped powers not conferred by the Constitution.
9. Because his party favors centralization, which is a step toward absolutism.
10. Because his government of the South is military rather than civil.
11. Because we have no assurance that a second term will satisfy him.
12. Because the old Know-Nothing element is unanimous in his favor.
13. Because his bungling Cabinet has brought disgrace on the national honor.
14. Because he has tolerated fraud and corruption to further his re-election.
15. Because he has fattened his impecunious relatives on the spoils of public offices.
16. Because his strongest partisans foster an antagonism of race, creed and section.
17. Because Civil Service Reform demands that Presidents should be limited to one term.
18. Because the honestest statesmen of the country are opposed to him.
19. Because the financial policy of the Administration favors stock-gambling.
20. Because he has done enough harm already.
21. Because he has bungled the Alabama Claims.
22. Because, though in 1868 his motto was "Peace", in 1872 he is the standard-bearer in the party of Hate.
23. Because his leading Orator has openly expressed a desire to have Grant made "Perpetual Dictator."
24. Because he is a Gift taker.
25. Because of his speeches . . .

AN AMERICAN VIEW OF IRISH-AMERICAN NATIONALISM, 1872.

Source: "The Editor's Easy Chair," Harper's New Monthly Magazine, July, 1872.

Is there any nationality which has become so entirely a passionate romantic sentiment as the Irish? The largest halls will be crowded by the most rapt and enthusiastic audience to hear a fervid orator denounce the invader and despoiler, and prophesy that from her ruins and her desolation Erin will rise again triumphant. It is a faith even more actual and intense than that of the Israelites in their restoration. Traditionally they wait with their hearts turned toward Zion and the Holy City. One day, they say, all the tribes will be gathered again, and the chosen people shall be supreme. But they make no raids upon Palestine. They throw no banners to the breeze at the Hebrew headquarters in foreign cities. They do not march annually in solemn procession and shake metaphorical fists at abstract tyrants, and kindle with tearful enthusiasm as the legends of Tara and the Druidical hill, of Patrick and the monasteries, are fondly repeated.

That story of the royal residence upon the hill of Tara; the pavilion here, the summer palace there; the proud coronation of Brian Boru as king of united Ireland; the coming of Patrick, saint of the sunny life; the declaration of the Druids that he spake truth; the prostration of the queen in recognition of his Divine mission -- all this imposing tale, recited a hundred times in every form of rhetoric, is as familiar to every Irishman as the news of the morning to the diligent reader. There is no spectacle more interesting than that of the Irish throng hanging upon the words of an Irish orator as he tells the old tale. They are all sure that Ireland was once the calm seat of a lofty civilization, the chosen land of religion, the mother of arts and learning. Soft and fair were the fields of their native land; stately and beautiful the temples that a pure faith builded; peaceful, frugal, and industrious the people that tilled the fertile soil, and whose voices filled the air with the sound of prayers and of hymns of adoration.

As the impassioned orator proceeds, the picture becomes more vivid and alluring. The sympathetic crowd behold with fascination. If the speaker be a priest, still more a friar in the garb of his order, most of all if he be a Dominican or a Franciscan, whose ministry first combined in theory the virtues of the cloister with those of society, how profound is the attention! All lands dwindle before the historic reality of Ireland, which they hear described, and what nation to-day rivals that ideal nation which was old when Rome was new -- the nation to which they belong!

"It is my land," fervently exclaims the orator, "my native land! I am born of that race, so intensely peculiar -- one of the master races of the world! My fathers, your fathers, were the spiritual children of Saint Patrick. It is our faith that has maintained our nationality. Often all has perished but that; but while that remains Irish nationality is indestructible. Of all nations the most Christian at its first conversion, the most Christian still. For what were the three chief characteristics of the founder of our religion but poverty, chastity, and obedience? These were the vows of the monastic orders. By these the Christian character was most fully developed. And these are the characteristics of my countrymen to-day!"

Not the sanctity of the temple restrains the applause. That eager multitude, hard-working men and women, of little education, sit or unconsciously rise as they listen, and revenge themselves upon the cruelty of fact by delight in that illimitable fancy. Yet the orator has few charms, and little real eloquence. His voice, indeed, is full and manly, but it has little music, nor is his action graceful, nor is his oration lit with imagination. But he certainly gives you a fresh impression of the intensity of the Irish national feeling. "The Danish invaders found as they landed on Irish soil what I wish every other invader had found -- a grave." They are not startling words from an Irishman to Irishmen; but they are strange to hear from one calling himself a Christian minister standing before a Christian altar. Yet they are spoken with a feeling which seems the more sincere when he adds, "I preach no rebellion, nor do I pretend to hate Englishmen, among whom I have true and beloved friends."

That remark showed how purely a sentiment the Irish nationality has become. It has virtually ceased to be a cause. For the raids which they make are of small proportions and upon a distant soil, and the headquarters from which banners are flung to the breeze are far, very far, from the hill of Tara. The splendors of a civilization all traces of which have perished, the docile innocence of primitive people which the ardent imagination can readily picture, a universal goodness and power and supremacy and happiness which nobody can disprove more than he can prove, all lift the argument into the realm of twilight and shadows and romance. If there were a great civilization here, did it not perish in conflict with a greater? In the course of history do the more powerful influences succumb to the weaker? If, as the orator declares, it is his Church which has maintained the nationality of Ireland, how has it maintained it? Has it made the people intelligent and prosperous? Has it freed them from superstition, and broken all spiritual shackles? Has it taught them the arts of industry, and preached peace and good-will? It has been wickedly persecuted, no student will deny; but did it never persecute? The power of its priesthood has been almost absolute. But responsibility is commensurate with power. How has it discharged that responsibility in elevating its people?

These are the questions that follow in the mind on many a hearer the sad words of the orator. "The greatness of my country is seen in her ruins," he says, with a feeling to which the sensitive heart of the audience thrills in response. But what are those ruins? Are they buildings only? Are they only the round towers, the cromlechs, and the mossy stones of fallen monasteries? What constitutes a state, O fervent father? And what is that which, while it remains, may smile at all other ruins? If you ask us to see Ireland in its ruins, we may look and discover warmth of feeling, generosity, genius, the qualities of a historic race; but we shall look for them elsewhere than on the hill of the druids or among the foundations of Armagh.

As he ends, the orator turns toward the altar for a moment; then, putting his hand under his Dominican robe, he descends the steps and disappears from the church. The organ fills the air with the pathetic melody which Moore's song has made familiar:

"The Harp that once through Tara's halls
The soul of music shed."

The audience, delighted for an hour and a half, rises and pours out at the doors, every one prouder that he comes of a nation which built the round towers, and which furnished the most learned scholars of the Middle Ages. It has not been a discourse which rooted them faster in the land which they have chosen for a home and for their children's country. Its moral is two-fold: First, that the English invaded Ireland, sought to obliterate its nationality by every monstrous means, and are the authors of its long misery, and second, that the nationality will endure only so long as the dominant form of religious faith in Ireland remains unchanged. But the cultivation of an aimless traditional hatred is certainly worse than useless, and mere sentimental passion is fatal to vigorous character.

It would be well if orators who come to us from abroad would remember that any appeal to any part of the population of this country which tends to destroy its homogeneity is a little impertinent. The condition of the true power and permanence of the American nation is assimilation, not aggregation. A great nationality will spring from intimate union and transfusion, not from patching and confederating. The instinct of union is not partisan or local, it points to the necessary law of national existence and development. Real union is delayed and a genuine nationality is impossible so long as we rally in different clans with no common slogan. In other days, when an American traveler entered his name upon the book of a hotel by some Italian lake, or far up a Swiss valley, as from Virginia or Texas, the little fact had a significance which really involved civil war. Akin to the feeling which made that entry is the division of American citizens by the names of other countries, and the appeal sometimes made in politics to this vote or to that vote. How will the Germans go? How will the Irish vote? are questions which really imply that they are not Americans, and therefore ought not to vote at all.

The audience which the fervid orator of whom we have been speaking addressed was an American audience. It was, indeed, largely composed of citizens who were born in Ireland, or who were descended from Irish ancestors. But if the hearer waited to hear them exhorted to reproduce in their chosen new country the virtues which the orator described as distinguishing their ancestors in the old, he listened in vain. They were told of the isle of saints, of the scholars, of the seats of learning full of men devoted to temperance and all the virtues. But let the hearer remember what the orator forgot to say -- that the same virtues and the same education and intelligence would make their new country greater than their old. They were told that their form of religious faith had preserved their nationality. But let them not forget that they have changed their nationality, and that here all forms of religious faith are equal. Messieurs, the orators may cry resurgam, and prophesy the restoration of the grandeur and the glory of Tara and of Armagh. But what then? We are Americans.

AN IRISH-AMERICAN VIEW OF ENGLAND, 1874

Source: The Irish World, September 19, 1874.

. . . Here now is the position of England. With all her colossal power, she dare not move. She dare not, upon any consideration, make war against Germany, or Russia, or the United States. A war between England and the United States would be the ruin of England. A fleet of half a score of Irish-manned privateers would in six months sweep the seas of English commerce! We know what a few English-built privateers did to American commerce. The effect is felt to this day. This Republic, however, is so vast in extent of territory, it embraces such a diversity of climes, and it is so rich in internal resources, that its population could get along forever without interchange with other nations. It is, in fact, a world in itself. With England it is otherwise. Her territory is very small. Her population is proportionally very numerous. Manufacturers are her labor, and commerce is her profit. The world is her market. Destroy her commerce, and you destroy also her manufacturers. What is the result? Famine followed by civil war, in which the monarchy would be demolished, the aristocracy forever swept away, and her world-wide possessions cut loose and forever independent of her sceptre! This would be the result of a war between England and the United States. England knows this well. Therefore England will take good care to engage in no such war. Her great battles are all fought.

But if England does not wish to make war -- and because she is not in a position to make war -- it is your business, Irish revolutionists, to create complications for her. You watch the long-looked for "opportunity". That is right. But it is your duty, too, to make that opportunity. Be active and vigilant. Your power is great. Your organizations are established in the United States, in Canada, in Ireland, and in England itself. No struggling nationality ever before ever had so many auxiliaries. No tyrant ever before ever had so many and widespread adversaries. Till now -- till this very generation in which we live -- Ireland itself had never any standing military organizations, the sole object of whose existence is her emancipation. You faint-hearted sons of the Motherland, be cheered! Lift up your hearts! You leaders and champions of the Irish cause, prepare for action! Do nothing precipitate, though. Don't be led away by impulse. But "in time of peace prepare for war."

This country is Ireland's base of operations. Here in this Republic-- whose flag first flashed on the breeze in defiance of England -- whose first national hosts rained an iron hail of destruction upon England's power -- here in this land to whose shores English oppression exiled our race -- we are free to express the sentiments and to declare the hopes of Ireland. It is your duty, revolutionary chieftains, to realize these hopes! If you are but true to this duty -- if you are but true to nature -- there are those among you who, perhaps, will yet live to uplift Ireland's banner above the ruins of London, and proclaim with trumpet-tongued voice, whose echoes shall reverberate to the ends of the earth, -- "The rod of the oppressor is broken! Babylon the great is fallen."

PARNELL ADDRESSES THE HOUSE OF REPRESENTATIVES, FEBRUARY 2, 1880.

Source: Congressional Record, 46th Congress, 2nd Session, Pt. I, p.664.

When the task is thrown upon America of feeding a people who have been driven into starvation by ruinous and unjust laws, surely you acquire a right to express your opinion very freely on the character of those laws and on the policy of maintaining them. And I have every confidence that the public sentiment of America will be a great assistance to our people in their present effort to obtain a just and suitable settlement of the Irish land question.

Since I have been in this country I have seen so many tokens of the good wishes of the American people toward Ireland that I feel entirely at a loss to express my sense of all the enormous advantage and service which is being daily done in this way to our cause. We do not seek to embroil your Government with the government of England; but we claim that the public opinion and sentiment of a free country like America is entitled to find expression wherever it is seen that the laws of freedom are not observed . . . .

It will be a proud boast for America if, after having obtained, secured, and ratified her own freedom by sacrifices unexampled in the history of any nation, she were now, by the force of her public opinion alone, by the respect with which all countries look upon any sentiment prevailing here, if she were now to obtain for Ireland, without the shedding of one drop of blood, without drawing the sword, without one threatening message, the solution of this great question. For my part, I, as one who boasts of American blood, (loud and long continued applause,) feel proud of the importance which has been universally attached on all sides to American opinion, with regard to this matter, and I am happy in seeing and believing that the time is very near at hand when you will be able to say you have in the way I have mentioned, and in no other way, been a most important factor in bringing about a settlement of the Irish land question.

AN ATTACK ON "BOSS KELLY" OF TAMMANY HALL, 1880.

Source: Editorial in the New York Herald, October 24, 1880.

But this Kelly will find that American opinion is not to be put down in that way. Irishmen who, like Kelly, are without the tact and sense that is the natural endowment of Irishmen with brains, but who have all the faith in bellowing and roaring and vindictive speeches that is equally an endowment of the more brutal of the breed, may imagine that what resists them in its characteristically still and temperate way yields before them, but if they do, they indulge in a vain fancy and since this champion of Irish and Catholic dictation seems to wish this issue to be made -- since he wants it understood that his way must be supreme, and that whoever objects shall be overwhelmed, if possible, by a deluge of vile names raked from the cesspools of his imagination or the yet fouler recesses of his memory-- he can have the issue made just as distinctly and clearly as the case may require. For when a Catholic Irishman, the leader of the Irish Catholic party, announces and boasts that he will decide political conflicts in this neighborhood as suits his good pleasure by means of the suffrages of thirty thousand Irish Catholic voters upon whom he can count, the people have an opportunity to see just what sort of an institution the Catholic church is in politics and to understand what a farce it would be to pretend that free government can continue where it is permitted to touch its hand to politics, or, indeed, to exist, for where it exists, it will not leave politics alone. This is a Protestant country and the American people are a Protestant people.

AN ATTACK ON IRISH-AMERICAN CLAIMS TO A ROLE IN AMERICAN HISTORY, 1887.

Source: "Notes and Comments" in The North American Review, vo. 145, no. 369 (June, 1887).

With one glance at Feneuil Hall, and the Irish "love of liberty" that would prevent Englishmen from using it in polite and harmless celebration of "Queen Victoria's Jubilee," permit me to correct the public misapprehension that the Irish were of any great and special service to this republic of ours, in the days of the Revolution. Among Irish-Americans and the politicians who court their votes, the claim of such service usually comes up at public meetings about as follows:

> "Ill would it become us to turn a deaf ear to the cry of suffering Ireland when we remember how, in the hour of our own travail -- in the hour when our own country was coming into the world amid roar of cannon and groans of anguish -- it was Ireland that held out to us the hand of fellowship, etc., etc."

Those who read the papers doubtless remember many orations framed upon this model. Sometimes the speaker goes farther, and attempts to particularize; and then we see something like the recent effort of a Massachusetts statesman and ex-governor who, in recounting the benefits received, says: "She sent us Montgomery!" and also remarks with unconscious humor, "Remember the memorial which Congress addressed to Ireland!" He does not give Ireland's response, but leaves us to believe that a beggar is indebted to him if he asks for alms, even though no alms be forthcoming.

Now, let us look, first, at the individual cases of prominent Irishmen in the Revolution.

There were soldiers of fortune from almost every country in Europe, who thronged to the revolutionary army, even to the extent that Congress was seriously embarrassed to provide offices for a host of applicants who looked for nothing less than major-generalships and separate commands. Among these there were doubtless Irishmen, but unfortunately for the force of the demagogues' plea, we do not find that our Irish auxiliaries were unmitigated blessings. They cannot point to a single name like Lafayette, Kosciusko, Pulaski, or Steuben; but there was Conway, whose restless, scheming spirit, and selfish treachery, well nigh imperiled the cause of liberty, and whose conspiracy to degrade Washington, to drive him from the service with a blackened reputation and to install the shallow Gates as commander-in-chief of the American army is registered in history as "Conway's Cabal." Fortunately the attempt failed.

I do not include the name of Richard Montgomery, the name that is most often quoted by the Irish panegyrist -- first, because he did not come here to assist us, but was a resident in the colonies before the war broke out, and second, because, though born on Irish soil, he was certainly not an Irishman. His name alone discloses his Scotch lineage, and, as a matter of fact, he was a descendant of one of Cromwell's settlers -- one of that class upon whom the vials of Irish wrath are ever emptied, and who, as Macaulay informs us, would resent the name "Irish" as a deadly insult.

I must be pardoned for mentioning, also, the historical circumstances that the soldier who, for an English bribe, undertook to poison George Washington, was an Irishman. But I have no wish to dwell on this part of the subject. It is not just to charge the acts of isolated individuals against their race, any more than it is just to credit to the race the virtues of stray individuals.

And now for a few hard facts which really bear upon the issue, -- only a few out of many, but enough to explode forever the fiction of American indebtedness to Ireland on the score of revolutionary succor.

In the first place, as to the disposition of the rank and file of Irish immigrants, I quote from Bancroft's "History of the United States," Vol. X., page 175 (first octavo edition):

"While it was no longer possible for the Americans to keep up their army by enlistments, the British gained numerous recruits from immigrants. In Philadelphia, Howe had formed a regiment of Roman Catholics. With still better success, Clinton courted the Irish. They had fled from the prosecutions of inexorable landlords to a country which offered them freeholds. By flattering their nationality, and their sense of importance attached to their numbers, Clinton allured them to a combination directly averse to their own interests, and raised for Lord Rawdon a large regiment, in which officers and men were exclusively Irish. Among them were nearly five hundred deserters from the American army."

So much for the spirit of the Irish immigrants.

Now let us see about the sympathy of the Irish in Ireland.

In 1779 the Spanish government, then at war with England, sent an emissary, a Catholic priest, to see what could be done in the way of creating a diversion in Ireland to aid the cause of the allies in Europe and America. Bancroft speaks of his mission as follows:

"He could have no success. After the first shedding of American blood in 1775, one hundred and twenty-one Irish Catholics, having indeed no formal representative authority, yet professing to speak not for themselves only, but 'for all their fellow Roman Catholic Irish subjects,"had addressed the English Secretary in Ireland, in proof of their grateful attachment to the best of kings, and their just abhorrence of the unnatural American rebellion,' and had 'made a tender of two millions of faithful and affectionate hearts and hands in defense of his person and government in any part of the world.' "

My references are Bancroft's "History," Vol. X., page 252, and Froude's "The English in Ireland," Vol. II, page 176.

Now turn to Ireland as represented in her Parliament; for she had a Parliament of her own then. I quote again from Bancroft, Vol. X., page 453.

> "When the tidings from Lexington and Bunker Hill reached them (the Irish), their Parliament came to a vote that 'they heard of the rebellion with abhorrence, and were ready to show to the world their attachment to the sacred person of the King.' Taking advantage of its eminently loyal disposition, Lord North obtained its leave to employ four thousand men of the Irish army for service in America. That army should by law have consisted of twelve thousand men; but it mustered scarcely more than nine thousand. Out of these the strongest and best, without regard to the prescribed limitation of numbers, were selected, and eight regiments, all that could be formed, were shipped across the Atlantic."

This, it may be said, was the act of the Irish Parliament as a whole. But to close the last loophole of doubt, let us examine the position taken by the Irish patriots, with Henry Grattan at their head. Bancroft again says, on page 454:

> "When, in 1778, it appeared how much the commissioners sent to America had been willing to concede to insurgents for the sake of reconciliation, the patriots of Ireland awoke to a sense of what they might demand . . . . At the opening of the session of October, 1779, Grattan moved an amendment to the address, that the nation could be saved only by free export and free import, or according to the terser words that were finally chosen, by free trade. The friends of government dared not resist the amendment, and it was carried unanimously. New taxes were refused. The ordinary supplies, usually granted for two years, were granted for six months. The house was in earnest, the people were in earnest . . . Great Britain being already taxed to the uttermost by its conflict with America, Lord North persuaded its Parliament to concede the claims of the neighboring island to commercial equality."

Here we have the patriot party of Ireland signalizing the American revolution, not by sympathy, not by aid, but making use of the occasion for obtaining advantages for themselves in return for the resources they furnished England to help suppress the cause of American independence! Comment is entirely unnecessary; and, while, perhaps, we should not blame them, under the circumstances, for the course they took, yet when they claim our gratitude for it, they exhibit an ignorance or an impudence for which they should occasionally, at least, be snubbed. There may have been isolated instances of Irish sympathy with "the spirit of '76," which I have been unable to discover; but it would require a long list of them to weigh much against the recorded facts. Let us hear somewhat less of the "debt to Ireland," save, of course, from the lips of the Irish agitator or American demagogue. By giving to the Irishman or German praise which has not been earned, we belittle the gratitude which we do owe to one and only one European race, for aiding our American Revolution. To France as a nation, and to the French as individuals, we are deeply indebted; and those who, for political capital, harp other names and display other flags, should remember that by so doing they insult the country to which America owes most but whose citizens are not here in sufficient numbers to incite the politician to defend their merits.

Duffield Osborne.

AN IRISH-AMERICAN COUNTERATTACK, 1887.

Source: "Notes and Comments" in The North American Review, vol. 45, no. 370 (Sept. 1887).

Irish Aid in the American Revolution

The Queen's Jubilee year has had many surprises for the Irish race the world over, but none so strange as the information afforded the American section of the children of the Gael in the July issue of the North American Review, which Mr. Duffield Osborne concludes is sufficient "to explode forever the fiction of American indebtedness to Ireland on the score of revolutionary succor.'' Most Irish-Americans had hitherto believed otherwise, even to the extent of doubting with ''the demagogues'' the truth of Mr. Osborne's oracular: "We do not find that our Irish auxiliaries were unmitigated blessings." It might be asked, what depth of historical research made Mr. Osborne a plural of sufficient weight "to correct the public misapprehension that the Irish were of any great and special service to this republic of ours in the days of the Revolution?" Indeed, a glance at his corrective contribution merely shows that he is fresh from the perusal of the pages of Mr. Froude, and entirely too guileless to perceive that, unfettered by the four corners of hard matter of fact, his historian is a past-master in the pleasing art of realistically romancing -- to borrow from Punch's parliamentary vocabulary.

Mr. Osborne looks first at "the individual cases of prominent Irishmen in the Revolution," and kindly admitting that among the "soldiers of fortune" who thronged to the revolutionary army "there were, doubtless, Irishmen,'' he can find no ''single name like Lafayette, Kosciusko, Pulaski, or Steuben," except Conway of "the cabal," over whom he waxes wroth. Mr. Osborne seems to be unaware that Conway was one of the soldiers from France of whom he is enamored, or that he was a mere tool, ''imprudently led into the cabal," as General Sullivan said in his letter to Washington, to further the jealous ambitions of the un-Irish clique headed by Gates, Mifflin, Schuyler, and Lee, who made him the scapegoat of their intrigue. He also conveniently ignores Conway's manly apology and regret for the part he took in the affair. If Mr. Osborne means that there were no trained Irish generals like Lafayette and his brother commanders, the explanation is easy. Ireland then, as now, was a nation of disarmed men, ground as far into the dust as the penal laws could force her. Where could commanders spring from such a source? But, even with this disadvantage, there are some single Irish names that stand out in American history on a par with those Mr. Osborne has mentioned. On the theory, I suppose, that being born in a stable does not make a man a horse, the name of Richard Montgomery is stricken off the roll of Irishmen, although he was born in "Dark Donegal," and his father was a member of the Irish Parliament. Granting this style of reasoning to Mr. Osborne, he must allow me the same privilege, and he will then be confronted by the "single names" of such Irishmen born in America as Major-General John Sullivan and his brother James, Major-General Henry Knox, Major-General Anthony Wayne, Major-General James Clinton, and Major-General John Stark in the army; Jeremiah O'Brien, and his four stalwart brothers, sons of Maurice O'Brien, of Cork, the heroes of "the Lexington of the Seas;" or among the signers of the Declaration of Independence with the names of George Read, Thomas McKean, of Delaware; Charles Carroll, of Carrollton, Md., Thomas Lynch, of South Carolina; and Thomas Nelson, of Virginia, whose grandfathers were Irish born; and Edward Rutledge, of South Carolina.

If he does not like this turn and wants to hear of native-born Irishmen like Montgomery, let him hunt up the histories of Generals Stephen Moylan, Edward Hand, William Thomson, Walter Stewart, William Maxwell, Griffith Rutherford, John Fitzgerald, Washington's favorite aid; Commodore John Barry; or among "the Signers," of James Smith, and George Taylor, of Pennsylvania, and Mathew Thornton, of New Hampshire. These are "a few of the hard facts which really bear upon the issue -- only a few out of many, but enough to "explode forever" Mr. Osborne's fiction of the absence of American indebtedness to Ireland on the score of Revolutionary succor.

In answer to the assertion that a drunken vagabond of an Irishman was bribed to poison Washington, it can be said there was also an Arnold, and, to disapprove any reflection on the race by the former fact, it is recorded that when Arnold's treason was discovered, the picked men of the whole army sent by Washington to guard West Point were the "Pennsylvania Line," Irishmen nearly to a man, as their muster rolls prove.

To show the "spirit of the Irish immigrants," Mr. Osborne cites from the not unprejudiced or reliable pages of Bancroft, that Clinton raised for Lord Rawdon "a large regiment in which officers and men were exclusively Irish. Among them were nearly five hundred deserters from the American Army."

Well, what if he did. The Tory Joseph Galloway, a native of Pennsylvania, in his testimony before the House of Commons in 1779, stated that he had received in Philadelphia, from the army at Valley Forge, 3,000 deserters; and Sabine, in his "History of the Loyalists of the American Revolution," says: "I conclude that there were, at the lowest computation 25,000 Americans who took up arms against their countrymen, in aid of England." This proves "the spirit" of the army and of the country at large in the same ratio as Bancroft's "large regiment" does for the Irish immigrants. What are the real facts? In the Parliamentary investigation above quoted, Galloway again testified, in answer to the question of the army enlisted in the service of the Continental Congress: "The names and places of their nativity being taken down, I can answer the question with precision. There were scarcely one-fourth natives of America, -- about one-half Irish, -- the other fourth English and Scotch" (vol. 13, page 431, British Commons Reports).

General Robertson, who had served in America twenty-four years, swore: "I remember General Lee telling me that he believed half the rebel army were from Ireland" (Id., page 303.)

Washington's adopted son, George Washington Parke Custis, says in his Personal Recollections:

"Tell me not of the aid we received from another European nation in the struggle for Independence. That aid was most, nay, all-essential to our ultimate success; but remember the years of the conflict that had rolled away; and many a hard field had been fought ere the fleets and the armies of France gave us their powerful assistance. We gladly and gratefully admit that the chivalry of France, led by the young, the great, the good, and gallant Lafayette, was most early and opportunely at our side. But the capture of Burgoyne had ratified the Declaration of Independence. The renowned combats of the Heights of Charleston and Fort Moultrie; the disastrous and bloody days of Long Island, of Brandywine, and of Germantown; the glories of Trenton, of Princeton, and of Monmouth, all had occurred; and the rank grass had grown over the grave of many a poor Irishman who had died for America, ere the Flag of the Lilies floated in the field by the Star Spangled Banner . . . .

"Of the operatives in war -- the soldiers, I mean -- up to the coming of the French, Ireland furnished in the ratio of a hundred for one of any foreign nation whatever.

"Then honored be the good old service of the sons of Erin in the War of Independence. Let the Shamrock be intertwined with the laurels of the Revolution, and truth and justice, guiding the pen of history, inscribe on the tablets of America's remembrance eternal gratitude to Irishmen!"

Perhaps Mr. Osborne will set this down, however, as coming from the lips of an "American demagogue."

The Marguis de Chasteloux, a distinguished Frenchmen, who was here in 1782, published an account of his travels. An English gentleman, in his translation of this novel, in a note to a friendly allusion to an Irish soldier of the Revolution, writes as follows:

"An Irishman, the instant he sets foot on American soil becomes ipso facto an American. This was uniformly the case during the whole of the late war. While Englishmen and Scotsmen were regarded with jealousy and distrust, even with the best recommendation of zeal and attachment to the cause, a native of Ireland stood in need of no other certificate than his dialect."

The "spirit of the Irish immigrants" was still further manifested in July, 1780, by an association in Philadelphia called the "Friendly Sons of St. Patrick," the members of which were either of Irish birth or blood. Twenty-seven of them subscribed, in gold and silver, to the relief of the starving patriots of the army, then at Valley Forge, the sum of one hundred and three thousand five hundred pounds, Pennsylvania currency. General Stephen Moylan was the President of this society, and the man whose generosity then saved the nation, bore such Irish names as Thomas Fitzsimmons, John and Matthew Mease, John Maxwell Mesbitt, John Shee, Blair McCleachan, and George Meade. If Mr. Osborne will accept the testimony of a "demagogue" named Alexander Hamilton, he will find him bearing witness to the help he obtained from Thomas Fitzsimmons, in establishing the financial policy of the Government and in funding the debt incurred in waging the Revolutionary War. The "Friendly Sons of St. Patrick" made George Washington an honorary member at their meeting, at which he was present, at the City Tavern, in Philadelphia, on January 1st, 1782. In accepting the membership, Washington wrote to the president of the society:

"I accept with singular pleasure the ensign of so worthy a fraternity as that of the Sons of St. Patrick, in this city, a society distinguished for the firm adherence of its members to the glorious cause in which we are embarked."

Another instance of "demagogery!"

In 1789, the Catholics of the United States, then almost exclusively of Irish birth or origin, presented an address of congratulation to Washington on his election to the Presidency. In his reply the first President said:

"I presume that your fellow citizens will not forget the patriotic part which you took in the accomplishment of their revolution and the establishment of their government."

All this hardly agrees with the "spirit" with which Mr. Osborne has tried to animate his "Irish immigrants," and he has had no better success with his "Irish in Ireland."

In order to draw a parallel, he cites from Bancroft again, and from Froude the alleged fact that "in 1775 one hundred and twenty-one Irish Catholics," in proof of their "just abhorrence of the unnatural American rebellion," made a tender to the English King of "two millions of faithful and affectionate hearts and hands in defense of his person and government in any part of the world."

Has Mr. Osborne ever heard of the powerful body known as the historical convocation of the "three tailors of Tooley street?" or, has he read, recently, in the public press, of the extraordinary manifestation of Irish National gratitude and rejoicing over Queen Victoria's "jubilee," as evidenced in the presentation to "Her Majesty," by a poor Irish widow, of two fresh eggs? Either of these incidents would be on a representative par with his alleged historical "petition." Besides, Mr. Froude has been challenged to produce this "petition," and has failed to do so. A few lickspittle "nobles" -- having as little in common with the Irish nation as have the Anti-Home Rulers, to-day -- did send a petition in 1775, to Sir John Blaquire, protesting their "loyalty" in terms of slavish and servile adulation; but there is not a single word about America in the copy that is extant.

Then Mr. Osborne, with that thorough insight into Irish history that distinguishes his whole article, next turns "to Ireland as represented in her Parliament; for she had a Parliament of her own then," he adds with unction; and tries to show that this Parliament voted soldiers to Lord North to put down the Revolution. He does not state (he probably does not know) that the Irish Parliament of those days did not have the right to originate any bill whatever, and was made up exclusively of a section of Protestants barely representing one-sixth of the population of the Island. Whatever voting was done was done by the government majority of place-holders, who were as representative of the nation as were the "one hundred and twenty-one Catholics" of Mr. Froude's "petition". There was not a single Catholic, Presbyterian, Methodist, or other "dissenter" eligible to a seat in the so-called Irish Parliament of that time. Not a single one of the three million Catholics in the land could vote for a Member of Parliament, or even for a parish beadle. Lord Chancellor Bowes, speaking in the highest court of law in Ireland at the time said officially:

"The law did not presume a Papist to exist in the Kingdom, nor could they breathe without the connivance of the government."

Chief Justice Robinson, in a similar declaration, said:

"It appears plain that the law does not suppose any such person to exist as an Irish Roman Catholic."

The Irish Parliament consisted of three hundred members, only seventy-two of whom were elected by the people, the rest being appointed by the Lord Lieutenant and a few of the Anglo-Irish nobles, who owned the land.

These are the people of Mr. Osborne's "petition" and his Parliamentary enemies of American liberty!

Yet he has the effrontery "to close the last loophole of doubt" by an attempt (again quoting from Bancroft) to make "the Irish patriots, with Henry Grattan at their head," appear as having neither aid nor sympathy for the American Revolutionists." Unless Mr. Osborne is invincibly ignorant, he will find by an examination of the Irish Parliamentary reports, or of Barrington's "Rise and Fall of the Irish Nation," that the exact contrary is the case. The Irish patriot leaders -- Yelverton, Hatch, Wilson, Hussey Burgh, Bushe Daly, Ponsonby, Newenham, Ogle, Fitzgibbon, Connolly -- are all on record in strong speeches in opposition to the government's sending of resources or troops "to help suppress the cause of American Independence." Grattan, in the terrible scoring he gave Flood, on this very subject, said:

"With regard to the liberties of America, which were inseparable from our own, I will suppose this gentlemen to have been an enemy decided and unreserved; and that he voted against her liberty -- and voted, moreover, for an address to send four thousand troops to cut the throats of the Americans; that he called these butchers 'armed negotiators,' and stock, with a metaphor in his mouth and a bribe in his pocket -- a champion against the rights of America, the only hope of Ireland and the only refuge of liberties of mankind."

Has Mr. Osborne ever read the speeches in favor of the justice of the American cause made by an Irishman named Edmund Burke? They say some things very pointedly in opposition to his theory.

Arthur Lee, the diplomatic agent in Europe of the Continental Congress, with Deane and Franklin, wrote home, in June, 1777, saying:

"The resources of our enemy are almost annihilated in Germany, and their last resort is to the Roman Catholics of Ireland. They have already experienced their unwillingness to go -- every man of a regiment raised there, last year, having obliged them to ship him off tied and bound; and most certainly they will desert more than any other troops whatsoever."

Plowden, in his history, says: "In Ireland the people assumed the cause of America from sympathy."

General Howe, writing to his government in 1775, expressing a preference for German troops, tells of his "great dislike for Irish Catholic soldiers, as they are not at all to be depended upon."

In a third volume of the "American Archives," an account given of the attempt of a Major Roache to get recruits in Cork, says: "The service is so distasteful to the people of Ireland in general, that few of the recruiting officers can prevail upon the men to enlist and fight against their American brethren."

In the English House of Commons, in 1775, Governor Johnstone said: "I maintain that some of the best and the wisest men in the country are on the side of the Americans; and that, in Ireland, three to one are on the side of the Americans."

In the House of Lords, in the same year, the Duke of Richmond stated:

"Attempts have been made to enlist the Irish Roman Catholics, but the Ministry know well that these attempts have proved unsuccessful."

The Congress of the United States, addressing the people of Ireland in 1775, said:

"Accept our most grateful acknowledgments for the friendly disposition you have always shown to us."

I have here cited a few "isolated instances of Irish sympathy with the 'spirit of '76,'" which Mr. Osborne was unable to discover. He wishes us to praise France for the help she gave. Does he know that among the soldiers she sent were several regiments of the Irish Brigade? or that at the siege of Savannah and at Yorktown, where the French contingent were specially prominent, among the officers who distinguished themselves were "Frenchmen" named Count Arthur Dillon, Col. Roche de Fermoy, Col. Hand, Col. Browne and Col. Lynch? If he has ever been in Savannah he must have seen the monument in one of the principal squares that commemorates the "isolated instance" of the Irish hero, Sergeant William Jasper.

To conclude this very imperfect record, I shall slightly alter one of Mr. Osborne's own sentences, and say of his assertions: Comment is entirely unnecessary; and, while perhaps we should not blame him, under the circumstances, for the course he too, (sic) yet when he claims that we ought to hear no more of this "debt to Ireland," save, of course, from the lips of the Irish agitator or American demagogue, he exhibits an ignorance or an impudence for which he should occasionally, at least, be snubbed. Like Dick Deadeye, "he means well, but he don't know." When he learns more of the real history of the country, he will have less to say. And I do not even despair of having him an Irish-American champion. Did not the study of Irish history make a Home Ruler of Mr. Gladstone? In the face of that conversion shall we despair of so ripe a historical scholar and investigator as Mr. Duffield Osborne? Perish the thought! But he must abjure Froude and Bancroft, at least on Irish topics.

Thos. F. Meehan.

SOME IRISH-AMERICAN SPOKESMEN, 1888.

Source: The North American Review, vol. 147, no. 382 (Sept. 1888), pp. 281-301.

IRISH COMMENTS ON AN ENGLISH TEXT

"The only time England can use an Irishman is when he emigrates to America and votes for free trade." --
London Times

The hatred of the Irish people for England, due to seven centuries of unparalleled oppression, has produced notable effects in the history of more countries than the two most interested. It has more than once been a factor in deciding the policy of great nations, and many decisive battles have been won by the vengeful valor it inspired. And yet its influence is generally exaggerated, both by too enthusiastic Irishmen and by English statesmen who cannot always see beneath the surface.

"In whatever corner of the world you find an Irishman, there you find an enemy of England," is a saying that has passed into proverb. It is a common boast among Irish Nationalists; English statesmen and writers make it a subject of frequent complaint. But, like most other assertions of a sweeping character, there is both truth and falsehood in it. Leaving the Irish loyalists out of account, it is true of the remainder, who are the vast majority, only in a limited sense. Strictly speaking, in fact, it is only true where there is a case of actual war between the country where the Irishman resides and England. And even in war it is not always true when the man is found on British territory.

Two thousand Wexford rebels formed the flower of Abercrombie's army which drove the French out of Egypt. The Light Division, which wrought such havoc among the French during the Peninsular War, was very largely Irish, and regiments composed exclusively of Irishmen contributed largely to the defeat of Napoleon at Waterloo. And all this time fervent prayers went up to heaven from every cabin in Ireland for Bonaparte's success, and Ireland's interests were clearly on the side of England's defeat.

While all Ireland was looking anxiously for news of a Russian victory in the Crimea, and Irish patriots in America were seeking Muscovite aid for an uprising in the old land, the Eighteenth Royal Irish, by a desperate charge, captured an outwork of the Redan and retrieved the credit of that disastrous day for England. To-day, when Ireland and England are engaged in a desperate struggle in which the interests of the peasant class are more deeply involved than in any previous contest, and when the Irish race throughout the world is practically united, twelve thousand Irish peasants' sons in England's pay constitute the force which is the instrument used to do the most effective work against the people's cause.

But soldiers and policemen, it will be said, are not thinkers. Driven by adverse circumstances into England's service, they become part of a machine, and discipline and the excitement and provocation of battle bring out their natural fighting qualities. But how is it here in America? Do men of Irish birth or descent in this country do anything to aid England's cherished policy or render her any real service? Is it true that "the only time England can use an Irishman is when he emigrates to America and votes for free trade"?

The statement as put in the quotation is not true, as the foregoing statements have shown, but it is nevertheless only too true that the great majority of Irishmen in this country have, for some years at least, been doing England's work without intending it or knowing they were doing it. This is true, not alone in regard to the question of free trade, but also in the case of other important questions. But for Irish votes -- the votes of men whose hatred of England and her policy is deep and ineradicable -- the English demand for free trade would not be met by the desperate efforts of the Cleveland administration to reduce the tariff, for Mr. Cleveland would not be President. If those efforts succeed the very Irishmen responsible for it will be among the first victims. The first effect of the success of Cleveland's free-trade policy will be the immediate reduction of wages, and as the vast majority of Irish citizens belong to the wage-earning class they will be among the first sacrifices offered up to English greed. Their relatives in Ireland largely dependent on trans-Atlantic aid in one of the most trying hours of their unfortunate history, will be left powerless and helpless at the feet of the Coercionist Government. England at one blow will thus impoverish her Irish enemies in America and paralyze the arm of patriotism in Ireland.

But for the same Irish votes and the recreancy of Irish politicians guided only by sordid personal interests, or cowed by threats of political ostracism, the most serious danger that has threatened the Irish national cause for many years would not now menace it. If the extradition treaty should pass the Senate, there is not an act of resistance to tyranny classed as a crime by an infamous coercion act that cannot be brought under its provisions, and England's heavy hand can be laid on the Irish exile in this country in the crowded city of the East, on the Western prairie, or in the depths of the Rocky Mountain mine. Coercion would be brought to the very door of the Irish citizen of the United States, and he would have the melancholy satisfaction of knowing that his own vote contributed largely to bring about that extraordinary state of things.

But for Irish votes the Fisheries treaty, the weakest surrender of American rights that ever disgraced American diplomacy, would not have been conceded to enable the most virulent, the meanest and most treacherous enemy of Ireland among living Englishmen to return home with an increase of power and prestige to be used for the injury of the cause which those who cast those votes hold dear.

It is evident, therefore, that the assertion that "the only use England can make of an Irishman is when he emigrates to America and votes for free trade," is only half a truth. England finds many other uses for him, and they include the whole line of English policy in this policy in this country, of which Mr. Cleveland's administration is the exponent and the chief instrument. But did the Irish voters who are responsible for this state of things deliberately contemplate such a result, and will they continue to play the role of cat's-paw for England? Most assuredly they did not contemplate it, and it becomes every day more probable that they will contribute very largely to the correction of the evil. Many thousands of Irish citizens revolted against the pro-British policy four years ago, and their numbers will be swelled by large accessions this year. As the issue becomes more clearly defined, they will be found among the most enthusiastic supporters of the broad American policy represented by the present Republican Presidential candidate, and those who adhere to old party lines will help to reinfuse a truly American spirit into the Democracy.

The issue of Free Trade and Protection was never clearly presented to Irish citizens of the present generation before. The broad and comprehensive foreign policy that they are led to expect from the election of Mr. Harrison they first saw outlined in the dispatches of Mr. Blaine, and it at once attracted many thousands of them, not, as the Mugwumps charge, that they expected it to eventuate in war with England, but because they believed it promised many benefits to the land in which their lot was cast. Republican administrations, from Grant's to that of Arthur, had not a foreign policy to attract them, and Irish-American citizens in England were allowed to be outraged without even a protest. On the other hand, the Democratic administrations before the war had acted with commendable spirit and promptitude in such emergencies, and it was natural for lifelong Democrats to expect adherence to party traditions as a result of a Democratic triumph. They did not realize that parties, as well as men, had changed -- they were not even aware of the change they themselves had undergone -- and they did not understand, as few other men did, the logical development of the tendencies given to both parties by the result of the war.

These things are beginning to dawn upon Irish citizens now, and the next few years will witness an enormous and a permanent change in their attitude towards the two great parties that struggle for the mastery of the Republic.

During the war it was England's policy to break up the Union. Not from love of the Southern people, but from hatred and fear of Democratic institutions and a desire to create a great market for her wares, the English aristocracy and mercantile classes wished to see the Southern oligarchy build up a great slave confederacy that would manufacture nothing. They aided it as they dared. While Irish Democratic soldiers flocked to the defense of the Union, the voice of Ireland rang out from crowded mass meetings, sending sympathy to the North, and warning England to keep her hands off.

To-day, when the industrial life of the Republic is menaced by a combination of the same hostile forces, enough of Irish citizens will be found to sever old party ties and rush to the defense of the country's true interests to place them out of danger for a generation, if not forever. They recognize that America's interests are their own, and that hatred of England and love of their adopted country unite for once in urging them to strong and vigorous action.

After next November, England will find very little use for an Irishman in America, the American people will respect him more than ever, and every European potentate, from the Czar of Russia to the Pope in Rome, will know that he is not a thing to be trifled with. In short, the status of the Irishman will be raised in America, and England's hope of crushing him in Ireland will vanish into thin air.

John Devoy.

It is true that Irishmen are not as useful to England as they have been. They cannot be relied on to carry England's flag over the parapets of war as enthusiastically as of yore. They bait the masters in Parliament who have been baiting them. And, crime of crimes, they are not as useful in starving themselves to pay rent to Englishmen of older or later birth as was their wont up to a decade ago. But their lack of usefulness does not end there. It was the custom of the Irish when they emigrated hither to scrape and save in the Land of the Free to help those left behind to pay the otherwise impossible rents. Then, indeed, an emigrating Irishman was sueful. He worked here under blazing sun or in snow and rain for "the little tyrant of his fields" in Ireland. Instead of this, the once useful Irish emigrant now furnishes funds to harry to English landlords year in and year out. He watches every move of English diplomacy and delights in setting his foot upon its neck when it serpentines near him. The London Times trusts that a remnant of the old usefulness may survive in the emigrated Irishman voting for free trade in America.

It is a vain hope. It was written, if we may guess at the foggy penetralia of the writer's misapprehensions, under the idea that the issue of the present presidential campaign was, what it is not, namely, between a total extinction of the protective tariff and keeping the tariff where it is.

The question is actually limited in this campaign to the extent to which the tariff should be modified as a means of reducing the surplus revenue of the federal government. The Democrats propose to cut off the surplus, partly by a reduction of the custom dues, so scaled they claim as not to endanger the country's industries, and partly by a reduction of the internal revenue. The Republican plan is to lower the tariff, but more sparingly than the Democrats, and to make a correspondingly larger cut in the internal revenue, even to sweeping it away altogether if necessary. There is no grave risk to American industry, no usefulness to England in either scheme.

For my part I see more good in a moderate reduction of the tariff and a great benefit in reducing the Internal Revenue which taxes commerce between the States.

As to specific schemes for dealing with the surplus I prefer Mr. Randall's to that of Mr. Mills. As the Republican Senate measure has not been made known at this writing, I cannot judge of it. All the tariff measures submitted or likely to be submitted will be found to recognize the protective factor as necessary to be preserved.

American manufactures are to be fostered or protected for the good of the entire nation, and not merely for the manufacturer who gets the profits, nor alone for the workmen or workwomen he employs at the lowest rate he can get them to work for. Variety of industry is what makes a nation truly self-sustaining. The protective tariff has undoubtedly helped and is helping to make in this respect our national life complete.

England reared her industries on Protection. She reached what she called "free trade" out of her necessities. She could not feed her manufacturing population cheaply and she repealed the corn laws or tariff on breadstuffs. The empty English stomach cried out, and England has ever since made a virtue of filling it. Characteristic of English cunning overlaid by English egotism it is to do this, and it is the top and bottom of her free trade "philosophy." Foxlike, having cut off her own no longer tail of a tariff, she urges every other nation to do the same. Our tariff is still needed to keep off flies, withal.

No American party could hope to live which would attempt to uproot at this juncture the present system, which has answered its purpose so well, and no party is attempting it. To modify it so as to fit it to the growing wealth of the country is a task worthy of the highest statesmanship.

It is, however, not the Treasury surplus only which menaces the present tariff. The trusts, those aggregations of the capital in entire industries, combined for the purpose of raising prices and doubtless of lowering wages, attack it on one hand. The migration hither of European labor of the cheapest kind attacks it on the other, for all the factors which drive wages downward, as they have been going down, will tend to make a high tariff a burden. In proportion as it is a burden it must be lowered, and the reduction under such circumstances will help no outside nation whatever. It will not be useful to England.

More and more labor is coming to America. Our great country will attract an enormous immigration for a hundred years to come. As it absorbed millions of Irish and German, it is absorbing Swedish, Italian, Bohemian, Hungarian, Russian and Polish millions, and will continue to absorb them. It will draw and is drawing the best workers from England itself.

A spirit of hostility to the later European immigrants has given rise to an outcry against "pauper labor" coming here. I do not join in it. I respect all labor. Irish labor in America was once branded as the labor of paupers; so Italian, Bohemian and Polish labor is to-day. These later comers will progress. The country lifts its laborers up as no other country in the world does. Every working arm and brain added to our population adds to our potentiality of controlling the markets of the world in all things which the country will produce. And this is America's commercial destiny.

Before arriving at that stage of power, a long battle will have been fought with our commercial rivals, of which England is the greatest; but they will go down one by one before the ever-growing industrial might of America. It will not be the victory of to-day or to-morrow, and it involves many now obscure and complex factors; but one sign by which we shall know when the time for a sweeping tariff reduction is at hand for us will be the imposition by England of import duties on our manufactures to save her own from utter extinction. The "fair-trader" of to-day in England is the forerunner of the English "high-tariff man" of hereafter, and he is coming.

England has been and will be in language and race the sister, but in commerce and politics the foe of America. Her coal and iron coming out of the earth almost side by side make her the most compact industrial force of her size in the world. But her limit is definite, and her commercial overthrow will awaken no pity -- incarnation of selfishness and greed as she has been.

She robbed and misgoverned Ireland to preserve its land to her aristocrats and its commerce to the English trading class. Every Englishman from the king to the peer, from the bishop to the beer seller, was pecuniarily interested in Ireland's misgovernment -- the king for his revenues, the peer for his rents, his offspring for the fat offices, the bishop for his tithes, the parson for his fat livings, the trader for his monopoly. Had America remained a colony, such would be the relation of Englishmen to her to-day. Unshackled and free of this hierarchy of tribute-takers, America has grown to be England's competitor and will presently be her master.

Irishmen here will be Americans in the struggle. England has taught Irishmen to hate her by oppressing them, and by hating them even when she could no longer oppress. If, as now seems probable, England, urged thereto by men of broad minds and deep sympathies, should give Ireland a fair measure of self-government to the strengthening and solidifying of the British Empire, this hatred will disappear from Ireland as it dies out in England, and will be as sensibly modified among the free Irishmen in America. But whether justice is done to Ireland or not, the commercial conflict between England and America must go on. It has no sentiment in it. Irishmen here may be expected to see as clearly as others, in any event, what is good for America and what would be "useful" to England.

The Irish-born citizen will now vote for the tariff. When the time is ripe for it, he, in common with the rest of the American nation, will vote the commercial death of England. If that will be "useful," England is welcome to it. The London Times, which on the Irish question presents the unpleasant spectacle of a blind worm turning in its own outgivings, is welcome to it.

If I have traveled over-wide in accounting for the faith that is in me in this matter, it is because as an American citizen I cannot close my eyes to all the facts as they appear to me, though perhaps some may expect me as an Irishman to settle the question off hand in sheer revolt of feeling against the cynical malevolence of an ignorant Englishman.

Joseph I. C. Clarke.

Well, no. "When an Irishman emigrates to America and votes for free trade" it is not "the only time England can use him." The other time is when he does not emigrate, is, by English free trade, compelled to "stand and deliver" all that he can produce; is left without the chance of a career, often without the means of existence, in Ireland; and is forced to prostitute labor, skill, courage or genius, sometimes his life, in building up a power that while robbing proclaims him a worthless savage, she has during these centuries, out of the goodness of her heart, been laboring, almost hopelessly, to civilize.

A very long time that other time has been. With the exception of the few happy years during which Grattan's Parliament and Volunteers prevented British free trade in his countrymen's lives and property, it has, in the main, continued from the day England first found herself able to impose her "system of economy" or robbery on Ireland at the cannon's mouth. It exists to-day, and will continue to exist, Mr. Parnell's agitation, all other agitations, Mr. Gladstone's proposed so-called parliament, and all such toy parliaments to the contrary, notwithstanding, until some such crisis in English affairs as will follow the advance of Russia Indiawards, or the continuance by America of the protective tariff, affords armed Irishmen, under some Phil Sheridan, their "opportunity" to get the British Government, bayonets and free trade, "bag and baggage," out of Ireland at once and forever. Then, and not till then, finding occupation and an honorable career at home, can Irishmen prevent England from using them.

It would require volumes, instead of a brief article, to recount the uses he has made of those hundreds of thousands of Irishmen, who, starved by her policy from home, have been forced into her blue jacket or red coat, to follow her drumbeat around the world, in her numberless plundering, marauding and robbing expeditions against unoffending and defenceless countries, tribes and peoples, as well as in her deadlier conflicts with her equals in war. Those who, from actual experience in the camp, march or battle-field, are familiar with the qualities of the Irish soldier, need not be told to what use he can be put. And, when we consider that, according to Major Butler, of the British army, the proportion of Irishmen in it, during its most eventful period, rose to sixty-six percent, we may well ask, what would England have been without them? What would her history in Canada have been had it not been Wolfe who met Montcalm on the Heights of Abraham? How different might have been her place on the maps of Europe, Asia, and Africa without the services of the Lawrences, the Napiers, the Goughs, and the Roberts. What, to-day, might have been her place among the nations had it been other than Wellington and his countrymen, who, with their fellow Celts, the Highlanders, withstood the legions of the Great Corsican until the coming of Blucher on that fateful day at Waterloo.

In cabinet, parliament, and diplomacy she has made frequent enough use of the countrymen of Burke, Sheridan, Palmerston, and Dufferin. In literature how often do we find Steele, Sheridan, and Goldsmith doing duty as "English" authors. In her halls of learning, journalism, marts of commerce, workshops, and great industries, Irishmen in great numbers labor, to her gain and the loss of their native land. The tourist sees at every port in Ireland steamers laden with cattle and produce for England, and wonders why a country that produces so much is always poor and often starving. The explanation is -- Through free trade England takes all the peasant produces, beyond a bare existence, and keeps him a helot. The Nationalist objects to the use she has made of the noblest of his race, of the hangings, burnings, pitch-capping, banishment, and imprisonment to which she had subjected the Father Sheehys, Wm. Orrs, Wolf Tones, Emmets, Mitchells, Meaghers, Kirkhans, O'Learys, and others who sought to end her blighting sway in Ireland. Everything goes out of Ireland, and nothing is returned. Her intellect, skill, energy, and resources are drained away to support England, without even acknowledgment. Against all this the Nationalist protests, and, further, demurs at being hanged for mentioning the matter and its remedy to his countrymen. All these uses has she been able to make of Irishmen through free trade, for be it known that the crime of England against Ireland has been the destruction of her industries. Compared with this the baneful effects of her wars, massacres, and penal laws upon the national life have been transient and ephemeral.

Over one hundred years ago Hely Hutchinson, an Irish Tory gentleman, founder of the House of Donoughmore, wrote a series of letters to His Britannic Majesty's Government on "The Commercial Restraints of Ireland." In direct and dignified, though respectful language, they point out how one after the other of Irish industries, the linen trade excepted, had been destroyed by English laws, and asks for their repeal. The book was bought up by the Government, as high as a thousand pounds sterling being paid for a copy, and burned. A copy of it, however, still exists in the Stephen Calwell Library of the University of Pennsylvania, and would afford instructive reading to those Irish-Americans who propose to vote for the English policy against the country to which they have fled.

It is needless to say that the obnoxious laws were not repealed until, in 1782, an independent Irish Parliament, supported by Henry Grattan's Volunteers and Napper Tandy's artillery, enacted protective tariff laws for the revival of Irish manufactures. The movement of Grattan, like the beginning of the American Revolution, was a revolt against the no longer endurable restraints of British free trade.

During her eighteen years of protection, Ireland enjoyed a period of unexampled prosperity, and advanced in manufactures more rapidly than any other country in Europe.

To-day the tourist in Dublin lingers to admire the magnificent public and private buildings, now mostly vacant, that during that glorious era arose under the magical influence of protection.

But the spoiler prevailed. In 1800, British gold and bayonets carried, through a corrupted Parliament, the dreaded "Act of Union." Irish independence and manufactures fell at one blow. The great patriot and statesman who raised could no longer protect them. He had "stood by their cradle," he now "followed their bier." English free trade could now work its wont -- factories closing, owners bankrupt, workmen flying, ruin everywhere, is the story from that day to this.

This much for the uses England has made of Irishmen elsewhere. We are not disposed to underestimate the value, to her, of Irish votes, for free trade, in America, in the past. We cannot overestimate their importance to her, in the future, in the combined attack she and the successors of the slave-holding oligarchy are now making upon the educated labor and industrial independence of these States. The supplying of works of handicraft to over sixty millions of people now here, and others to come; the destruction of a great and rising rival, who, by superior skill and fair dealing, will soon drive her from the markets of the two Americas; the continued existence of the, as present constituted, British Empire, which, resting upon, must go down with the loss of manufacturing and commercial supremacy -- these are the colossal prizes for which she contends, these the nuts she expects to get out of the fire, by the use of her favorite cat's-paw, the Irish - American vote, when she modestly asks her professed enemies to elect to the Presidency the man who declares: "I believe in free trade, as I believe in the Protestant religion."

Will they do it? We think not.

Like that intense Irish Nationalist, the greatest of political economists, whose works are revolutionizing the world, Henry C. Carey, son of the Great United Irishman, Matthew Carey, friend of Washington and Lafayette, and co-laborer with Grattan, Irishmen in increased and increasing numbers are learning to be "always opposed to England, and therefore always right."

The subjoined extracts are from the Irish-American memorial presented to the recent convention that nominated General Harrison: "Believing that the good of our native can be best promoted by the greatness of our adopted country, and that its greatness will come through the success of the Republican party, under a leader worthy of the high office, an American of Americans, pledged only to the support of American principles, we are convinced that a larger number of our countrymen than ever before will labor with enthusaism to carry to victory the standard of that party over the first national convention of which Judge Robert Emmet presided."

William Carroll, M. D.

The above, like most statements of the London Times concerning Ireland and Irishmen, is not true. Unfortunately the Irish in their native land have been only too often used by England, and they have been among the most pliant instruments of British oppression in Ireland. The hated constabulary is mainly composed of Irishmen, while the paid magistracy, the judges and the various officers of the Crown, are drawn largely from the native element. It is true that these Government employes are renegade Irishmen, and that the higher officials are for the most part alien in race, religion and sentiment to the overwhelming majority of the people; but the facts are enough to disprove the statement that the only time England can use an Irishman is under the circumstances mentioned by the Times. However, considering the demoralizing system of bribes and corruption -- unparalleled in history -- which has been so marked a feature of English rule in Ireland, the only wonder is that a larger proportion of the people has not succumbed to the blandishments of the seducer.

As regards England's "use" of the Irish in America, it is undeniable that a large proportion of the latter have been and still are, unwittingly, no doubt, the tools of England. In so far as Irishmen in this country have supported the free-trade policy of the Democratic party, they have been virtually the allies and friends of England. Having lost her foothold in the European marts, and with Russia closely pushing her in the East, England turns wistfully to America in the hope of securing here a market for the disposal of her wares. Free trade would give her the coveted prise. There is no lack of evidence to show that one of England's most cherished desires is the triumph of the free-trade policy in the United States. The unanimous approval with which the English press of all shades of political opinion has hailed every free trade manifestation in the United States, such as the President's December message, the Mills bill and the Democratic national platform, speaks conclusively on this point. Neither have the English newspapers been backward in pointing out that the adoption of free-trade policy by the United States would give English manufacturers and English trade such a boom as they have not received during the present century.

Now it may be asked, Why cannot Irish-Americans see that by supporting the Democratic free-trade policy they are being used to further the interests of English manufacturers and English workmen, and that, too, to the sacrifice of the interests of American industries and American labor? This anomaly is easily explained. Until within a few years past almost the entire body of Irish voters were included in the Democratic party. How this came to be the case is well known to the student of American political history. It was the result of circumstances which every fair-minded man will now readily admit were beyond the conrol of the Republican party, and for which the Republican party, as a party, was not responsible. Indeed, it is a fact that in the days of Know-nothingism, which unscruplous Democrats have persistently represented as the offspring of Republicanism, there were far more members of that intolerant and un-American party drawn from the ranks of the Democracy than there were from the Republican ranks. The fact remains, however, that owing to a combination of circumstances which were entirely misunderstood by the Irish, the latter were almost in a body attracted to the Democratic party. The consequence was that the Democrats came to be regarded by Irishmen as their friends and the Republicans as their enemies, and a large number of Irish voters have ever since been too ready to accept unquestioningly the policy of the former party on any issue that might arise.

The Democratic party has been, moreover, glaringly disingenuous, inconsistent and even dishonest in regard to its attitude on the tariff. One time its leaders and party organs will loudly contend that the Democratic policy in regard to the tariff is one not of destruction, but of revision, and they make this contention in face of the fact that the party has for years been endeavoring to bring about, in a more or less direct way, an economic policy which even the members of the Cobden Club and the press of Free

Trade England---who certainly ought to be good judges in such matters -- characterize as free trade. At another time, when the above course would not be expedient, a virtually free-trade policy is openly espoused, while protection is denounced as the bane of the farmers. One story will be told to the wage-earners of the great manufacturing States, while a contrary story will be rehearsed to the people of the non-manufacturing districts of the South. This chameleon-like policy is beautifully illustrated in the glaring inconsistencies of the Mills bill. The Free Traders have thus succeeded in throwing dust in the eyes of many Democrats, Irish-Americans included. And to disarm any possible fears the latter might have lest England, the hereditary enemy of their native land, might be the principal beneficiary under the new economic system, it is always made to appear that such fears are utterly groundless, and that what in fact England most dreads is lest there should be a departure from the present protective policy?

These tactics have to a certain extent succeeded. But, on the other hand, the number of Irish-Americans who see the situation in its true light is increasing daily. It is safe to affirm that a large majority of the Irishmen who do their own thinking, and will not suffer others to do it for them, and who have, besides, no political axes to grind, have finally shaken off the yoke of the party bosses. The solid Irish-Democratic vote has been broken up forever, a result fraught with good to the country at large, and to none more so than Irish-Americans themselves. The wisest and best Irishmen among us, men not identified with either party, such as the thoughtful and learned Rev. Dr. Bernard O'Reilly, have hailed with joy this self-emancipating movement on the part of their countrymen. I think I can safely put the number of Irishmen in this State alone who have cut loose from their political bondage in the Democratic party as not less than one hundred thousand. It is needless to say that those voters cannot be used in the interests of England.

It is, however, a great mistake, and does Irish-Americans a gross injustice, to say that, as a body, their attitude in regard to a question like that of the tariff is governed solely or principally by the bearing of such question on English interests. Such is not the case. Irish-Americans in all matters pertaining to America are American citizens pure and simple, looking at American public questions from the standpoint of Americans, and joining faithfully and fraternally with their fellow citizens of all origins in furthering the interests of the Republic. Irish-Americans, while retaining their love for their native land, surely need not, and will not, on that account abate one jot or tittle of their Americanism. The primary objection of Irish-Americans to free trade is not that it would benefit their old enemy England --- though this result would be wormwood and gall to them -- but that it would injure America. And they favor the continuance of the protective system, not because it shuts out English goods from the American markets, though this result is most gratifying to them, but because it safeguards our own industries and the interests of our own workingmen. Intelligent Irish-Americans know that by voting against free trade they are not only serving the interests of the Republic but striking a most effective blow at England, and no true American will complain that they enjoy their sweet revenge on the hereditary enemy of both nations. Indeed, even a casual reader of the American press will see that in the present campaign Americans are scarcely one whit behind their Irish fellow-citizens in their hostility to England, and free trade is as roundly denounced by them because of the advantages it would confer on England as because of the injury it would inflict on America. This is only natural. England is the hereditary foe of America as well as of Ireland. Since the Colonies threw off the British yoke England has made two desperate attempts to destroy the Republic -- once in 1812, and again, in a far more treacherous and dastardly manner, during our Civil War. As a participant in the latter, I well remember the fierce indignation of our soldiers when gathering up on the battle-field the arms of the Confederate dead, at finding the weapons, in hundreds of cases, bearing the stamp of the British Crown. The first hostile shot fired on Sumter was from a gun forged in England. The "Alabama" and "Shenandoah," which inflicted upon American shipping a blow from which it has not yet recovered, were built in British shipyards, and in part manned by British seamen, with the avowed object of destroying our mercantile marine. Why, America has little less reason than Ireland to hate England, the deadly foe of both nations.

England is just now engaged in a third attempt to cripple the Republic by aiding the Free Traders to bring about an economic policy which would first destroy our industrial prosperity. I agree with the sentiments expressed on the floor of the United States Senate by that fearless and aggressive advocate of American principles, Senator Riddleberger, viz., that "we will never be a free nation until we have whipped England for the third time." Now, we have already whipped England twice, and the opportunity to administer a third drubbing will be presented the fall. This opportunity will be eagerly seized, especially by Irishmen, and although the instrument of castigation this time will be the ballot instead of the bullet, it will be found mighty effectual. Irishmen do not often get a chance to wipe out old scores with England, and, therefore, I feel satisfied that they will make the most of the present opportunity, and that thousands of Irish Democrats, throwing party obligations to the winds, will unite with their Irish Republican brothers in inflicting condign punishment upon the hated oppressor of their motherland.

M. Kerwin.

In this campaign the Irish-American voter has an important advantage over other voters. If he be a man of any intelligence he has had the opportunity for a study in comparative politics, which must be of great value to him in making up his mind whether Free Trade or Protection is the better policy for the country of his adoption. His own country is under the rule and tutelage of the great free trade nation, and for seven-eighths of a century it has enjoyed all those advantages which attend "buying in the cheapest market and selling in the dearest," without regard to the effects upon the producing classes, and which free trade offers us. The Irishman has had the opportunity of comparing theory with practice in this matter, and seeing whether the headlong race for cheapness is a blessing or a curse to "the most numerous class, that is the poorest."

And he knows by sorrowful recollection and recent observation that the outcome of it all is a national poverty, which Chinese Gordon declared to surpass that of the wretched and oppressed peoples of Asia and Africa he spent his life in trying to relieve.

The root of Irish misery -- as all impartial observers, free traders not excepted, are now coming to agree -- is to be found not in over-population, not in a bad land system, not in faults of creed or character of the Irish people, but in the absence of anything but farming to employ the people. The country feeds something like twice its population, and sinks into ever deepening poverty as emigration depletes the population yet further. If the land were divided among its people it would give them only $14.00 worth a head, and its ownership would not suffice to put a stop to perennial hunger and recurrent famine. The success of the Irish people as workmen, as farmers and even as capitalists in this country and in the British colonies, suffices to show that it is neither their creed nor their character which stands in the way of their prosperity at home. Between the closer study of the facts and failure of quack remedies there has been a steady approach to consensus on the nature of the evil. The only remaining difference is as regard the remedy. The Free Traders simply despair of the future of the island; Protectionists have a well-founded confidence that the method of protection to home industry, which lifted America from sinking into a similar slough in 1783-89, would be the economic salvation of Ireland.

The ruin of Ireland dates from the ill-fated Union of 1801. It was in the interest of British manufacturers that that Union was negotiated, although the rising of '98 furnished also a political motive. Napoleon had shut up the Continent from British exports, when they began to look to Ireland for an outlet for their surplus of manufactures. The first proposal of the Union in 1799 was rejected by the Irish Parliament expressly on the ground that it would involve the ruin of those Irish manufactures which had grown up under a protective tariff during the previous sixteen years. When they agreed to the second proposal in 1800, it was as Grattan said, the introduction of free trade. "All the policy," he said, "of nursing our growing fabrics, and thereby of improving the industry of our country, employing her children, and expending her wealth upon her own labor, is now abandoned, and the language of the Union is 'Buy where you can, and as cheap as you can.' " (Speech of March 19, 1800.)

Some reserves were made in the Treaty of Union in behalf of Irish manufactures, by the retention of some duties for a time, but by 1822 the last were repealed, and the manufactures did not survive them five years. The advantage of British manufacturers in the possession of large capitals, trained labor and well established markets, proved as effectual for labor and well established markets, proved as effectual for the extinction of Ireland's manufacturing industry in the nineteenth century, as vile laws had been for its suppression in the eighteenth. Hence the vast power acquired by her landlords and abused by so many of them of levying rack-rents upon the lands, and of confiscating the tenant's improvements by adding their annual value to the rent. Hence the desolating famines, which never fall upon countries whose manufactures give them the means to draw upon the resources of other land in the hour of need. Hence the ruin not only of tenants but of freeholders and landlords, by the prostration of their one industry through the absence of any home market for its products. Hence the flight of the people by millions from the country they love so passionately, to enrich other lands by the industry which found no opening at home. Hence the demand from the Irish people for the restoration of that legislative independence under which they prospered through the care taken of their industries by protective legislation, and which they would use to restore that legislation. "Protection is an article of faith in the economical creed of the great majority of Irishmen," says Mr. George Pellew, an American Free Trader who visited Ireland in 1887.

The Irish-American voter who has given any attention to the matter knows that this is what free trade has done for his native country. He knows that Ireland has been sacrificed to England's ambition to make herself the workshop of the world, and to hold all other countries on the level of producers of food and raw material for her consumption. He knows that so long as England continues to legislate for Ireland, the root of Irish misery will never be touched by any remedy she will consent to have tried. And he now is asked to help to subject the industry of his adopted country to the same oppressive competition which ruined that of the country of his birth. It is alike his personal interest and his attachment to his native land which co-operates with his loyalty to that of his adoption in forbidding him to adopt this course. The Irishman in America is very generally a wage-earner. The extinction of manufactures and the exhaustion of capital at home sent him to America to make his beginnings at the lowest round of the ladder. He had not even skilled labor to offer to his employers, for where could he acquire that in a country which imports nearly every spade and shovel, knife and fork, chair and table, boot and shoe, dish and plate, piece of paper, and woolen or cotton garment that is used in the island? This is the exhibit made of Irish industries in the testimony taken by Sir Eardley Wilmott's parliamentary committee in 1885. The utter want of any kind of industrial skill, its complete extinction through disuse, is a common subject of lament among all classes in Ireland.

As a consequence, the Irish in America, although now they are taking to farming in rapidly increasing numbers, and although many of them have risen to become employers of labor, are in the main wage-earners still. What have they of their class to gain by introducing into America the cheapness of Ireland, when this is sure to bring with it that depression of the producing classes upon which this cheapness depends? Are they oppressed by a tariff under which the wages of the skilled artisan have risen from four hundred and thirty-eight dollars to seven hundred and twenty dollars a year, while the cost of necessaries has fallen from twenty-six to forty-six per cent. -- a tariff which brings them in increased wages seven times as much as the higher cost of living in America takes from them? They are not so stupid as to risk their own welfare for the promotion of a policy which would insure chiefly to the benefit of the hereditary enemy of their country, and whose introduction is hailed with delight by all the organs of British opinion.

Some Irish-Americans will agree to all that can be said against free trade in both Ireland and America, but they refuse to see that it is an issue in American politics at the present time. They adhere to the Democratic party because they refuse to believe that it means to proceed further in the reform of the tariff than is needed to remove its inequalities. They are taken with such objections as that the Mills bill proposes nothing more than a reduction between a sixth and a seventh of the present duties. But they cannot but regard it as ominous of no good to the country that the organs of English opinion are so jubilant over the President's Message of January last and the Mills bill. It is a safe rule in warfare, whether military or industrial, to find out what your enemy wants you to do, and do not do it.

If the Mills bill proposed a horizontal reduction of one-sixth along the whole line, there might be a plea that it would not do much harm. But if a man tears down part of a wall to the very foundation on the plea that the whole wall was higher than was necessary for its purposes, he hardly can plead that his whole operation amounted to no more than a reasonable reduction of its height. As regards salt, wool, lumber and a number of important American products, whose production must affect the labor market and the welfare of our farmers, the Mills bill enacts absolute free trade. In other cases it makes reductions which put the duties much below the protective level. The amount of this reduction is made to appear less in the "between six and seven per cent." calculation, by reason of especial favors extended to Southern industries, like the growing of peanuts and sumac, and to Northern industries located in States whose votes are sorely needed by the Democrats this year.

It is especially important to note that the Mills bill is not regarded as a finality by any of its supporters. It is only, in the words the late Mr. Dorsheimer used of its predecessor, "the first firm step toward free trade"; or in those of Mr. Watterson, the first move toward "the total destruction of the protective system." He who votes for the Democratic candidate this year, expresses in his vote his approval of the doctrines of the President's Message, which involves one such bill after another until free trade is complete. And he also votes to fasten the hold of the free trade leaders upon the Democratic party, so that as long as that party has control of any department of the government, that control will be used in the interests of the free-trade policy. Let any intelligent voter place himself, in imagination, in the halls of Congress on the first Monday of next December, if Mr. Cleveland should be elected. What would be the atmosphere of the House in this matter? What the character of the proposals with reference to the tariff? Would these be confined to the Mills bill, bad as it is, or would not the free-trade leaders begin to "wonder at their own moderation" in proposing so mild a measure? It is impossible to see how a protectionist who is sincerely attached to the Democratic party and believes in its principles can do other than wish for its defeat this year, that the incubus of free trade leadership may be thrown off forever.

Robert Ellis Tompson.

ANNOUNCEMENT OF THE ORGANIZATION OF THE AMERICAN IRISH HISTORICAL SOCIETY, JANUARY, 1897.

Source: Journal American Irish Historical Society, I, 1.

. . . A number of gentlemen interested in the part taken in American history by people of Irish birth or heritage are about to organize themselves into an historical society for the purpose of investigating and recording the influence of that element in the up-building of the nation.

People of Irish blood have been coming to this continent, voluntarily or otherwise, since the date of its earliest settlement. While they have been a valuable addition to the colony and republic in all departments of human activity, their work and contributions have received but scant recognition from chroniclers of American history. Whether this omission springs from carelessness, ignorance, indifference, or design is now of little moment. The fact that such a condition does exist makes it imperative that it should be remedied, not only in the interest of historical truth, but of racial fair play. Certain elements in the make-up of the American people have not hesitated on occasion to masquerade at the expense of the Irish, in borrowed plumes, and to pose under plundered laurels. It is the duty of honest historians to look after the rights of the lawful owners.

The history of Irish immigration to this country is of profound interest. The motive that inspired this sturdy people in coming to these shores was largely the one that animated and inspired all immigration -- discontent with the existing home conditions, civil, religious, political, industrial, and the hope of living under better and nobler conditions here.

The American of English stock has his historical society, the descendants of the Dutch, Huguenot, and Spaniard have associations which specialize the historical work of the bodies they represent; and we feel that the story of the Irish element should be told before the mass of legend and fiction now flooding the country under misleading designations has completely submerged the true facts.

The work of our projected society will be influenced by no religious or political divisions, for with us the race stands first, its qualifying incidents afterwards. It matters little where the people came from, whether from the north, the south, the east or the west of Ireland. It is of minor importance in what church they worshipped; we wish merely to concern ourselves with the work done by them here; to record the story of their participation in the civil, military, and political activities of the land, and to try truthfully and fearlessly to record their achievements.

The Society now in the process of formation must, we believe, be made up of men who have the patience to search, the knowledge and vision to sift and discriminate, and the ability to place the results in acceptable literary form. Lastly, the character of the Society must be such that it will be accepted as having a definite historical value which can be used in general works treating of the growth of the republic by historians of a future date. This, in brief, is the project; it is ambitious, but it is worthy; it is absolutely necessary if the good name and influence of an essential, but much neglected, chapter in American history shall be perpetuated.

To place the Irish element in its true light in American history, to secure its correct perspective in relation to historic events on this soil, is the final aim of the new society. Its primal aim will be to ascertain the facts, weigh them in relation to contemporary events, and estimate their historical value, avoiding in this process the exaggeration and extravagance of poorly-informed writers on the one hand, and the prejudice and misrepresentation of hostile writers on the other.

The organization will be constructed on a broad and liberal plan. It will be non-political, and no religious test will be required for admission to membership or the holding of office. Being an American organization in spirit and principle, the Society will welcome to its ranks Americans of whatever race descent who evince an interest in the special line of research for which the Society is organized.

Some of the projectors belong to other historical bodies, and it was believed at first that the work for which this new society is to be formed could better be done through the medium of those bodies and without the necessity of a separate organization. Experience, however, has led to the conclusion that this is not so. Hence the resolve to form a distinct body, with its own special object, program, and mode of procedure.

There is a place for such a society in the community; its purposes are honorable and useful, and its work should begin while yet documents, records, and historical material are available. We feel that such a work will be valuable not only to the Irish race, but to the American race also, to whose fiber this element has contributed its share. . . .

RESOLUTIONS VOTED BY IRISH-AMERICAN CONVENTION IN NEW YORK CITY, MAY 14, 1917.

Source: The Gaelic American, May 29, 1917.

Whereas, the United States, according to the declaration of our honored President himself, has entered the European War to promote the cause of democracy and civilization, and

Whereas, the Allies have repeatedly proclaimed that they, too, are fighting for the same cause, and for the freedom of small nations, and

Whereas, the British Premier stated under date of April 27, 1917 that "the settlement of the Irish Question is essential to the peace of the world and essential to speedy victory in the war" . . . . Now, therefore, be it

Resolved, that this assemblage of American citizens of Irish blood, loyal to the United States, and ready to defend her honor and interests, and recognizing that our Government is entitled to the best advice that Irishmen who understand the situation can give, urgently request the President and Congress to demand that England make good her promises in the only way possible in regard to Ireland, namely by according to the Irish people their indubitable right to be regarded as a sovereign people, and by granting to Ireland full national independence . . . , and be it

Resolved that we therefore submit to the President and Congress that America's entry into the war for democracy and civilization gives our Government the right, and imposes upon it the duty, to demand from England that she settle the Irish Question permanently and finally . . . . Such a settlement would be of untold benefit to the preservation of the future peace of the world, and its accomplishment would be another glorious achievement by the United States.

AN AMERICAN "INVESTIGATING TEAM" REPORTS ON IRELAND, 1921.

Source: Report of the American Commission on Conditions in Ireland, New York, 1921, p. 55. (L. Hollingsworth Wood, Chairman; Frederick C. Howe, Vice Chairman; Jane Addams, James H. Maurer; Maj. Oliver Newman; Norman Thomas; Senator George W. Norris; Senator David I. Walsh, members.

Conclusions

We find that the Irish people are deprived of the protection of British law, to which they would be entitled as subjects of the British King. They are likewise deprived of the moral protection granted by international law, to which they would be entitled as belligerents. They are at the mercy of imperial British forces which, acting contrary both to all law and to all standards of human conduct, have instituted in Ireland a "terror," the evidence regarding which seems to prove that:

1. The imperial British Government has created and introduced into Ireland a force of at least 78,000 men, many of them youthful and inexperienced and some of them convicts, and has incited that force to unbridled violence.

2. The imperial British forces in Ireland have indiscriminately killed innocent men, women, and children; have discriminately assassinated persons suspected of being Republicans; have tortured and shot prisoners while in custody, adopting the subterfuges of "refusal to halt" and "attempting to escape"; and have attributed to alleged "Sinn Fein extremists" the British assassination of prominent Irish Republicans.

3. House burning and wanton destruction of villages and cities by imperial British forces under imperial British officers have been countenanced and ordered by officials of the British Government; and elaborate provision by gasoline sprays and bombs has been made in a number of instances for systematic incendiarism as part of a plan of terrorism.

4. A campaign for the destruction of the means of existence of the Irish people has been conducted by the burning of factories, creameries, crops and farm implements and the shooting of farm animals. This campaign is carried on regardless of the political views of their owners, and results in widespread and acute suffering among women and children.

5. Acting under a series of proclamations issued by the competent military authorities of the imperial British forces, hostages are carried by forces exposed to the fire of the Republican Army; fines are levied upon towns and villages as punishment for alleged offenses of individuals; private property is destroyed in reprisals for acts with which the owners have no connection; and the civilian population is subjected to an inquisition upon the theory that individuals are in possession of information valuable to the military forces of Great Britain. These acts of the imperial British forces are contrary to the laws of peace or war among modern civilized nations.

6. This "terror" has failed to reestablish imperial British civil government in Ireland. Throughout the greater part of Ireland British courts have ceased to function; local, county, and city governments refuse to recognize British authority; and British civil officials fulfill no function of service to the Irish people.

7. In spite of the British "terror," the majority of the Irish people have sanctioned by ballot the Irish Republic, give their allegiance to it, pay taxes to it, and respect the decisions of its courts and of its civil officials.

AN IRISH-AMERICAN CONGRESSMAN LOOKS AT BRITAIN, 1939.

Source: Congressional Record, 76th Congress, 2nd Session, vol. 85, pt. 2, pp. 1213-1215 (November 1, 1939).

MR. McGRANERY. Mr. Speaker, during the last World War, I served in the Air Force of the United States Army; and even in my small role I had a glimpse of the horror of war which will forever remain indelibly impressed in my memory. This recollection is constantly before me and in itself would impel me to do whatever would keep America out of war, whatever would safeguard peace for our country with dignity.

An examination of the Record of the months preceding America's entry into the last war disclosed that the United States was drawn into war as a result of Germany's attacks against American vessels and American seamen. It is apparent that the only way our country could again be made to participate in a world conflict would be by the repetition of similar attacks upon American ships bearing American citizens or by the unwarranted searches and illegal delays of our vessels such as they are being subjected to by England at this hour. Therefore, it is imperative that the Congress enact this legislation which would prevent American vessels from entering belligerent waters. Postponement of the passage of this act might mean perhaps another flint on which the spark of war could be enkindled, with consequences too terrible to be forecast at this time.

I shall vote for the present act because I am convinced that its strict prohibition against any American vessel entering belligerent waters and its provision for cash and carry will provide adequate safeguard -- indeed, a guarantee against the United States becoming embroiled in World War II.

It is the urgent duty of every Member of this Congress to keep our ships from entering zones of danger. Otherwise, we may be confronted with a situation similar to that of March 1917 when, in the words of Newton D. Baker:

> There was only one thing to do; or two, perhaps -- we could yield, or we could fight.

Mr. Baker, with clarity and intensity, set forth the difficult choice that remained to America, once her ships bearing her citizens had been ruthlessly attacked upon the seas.

The United States refused to yield, and so the youths of our great country were sent across the seas to fight. The Gold Star Mothers can tell better than we the epic of the gallant and tragic end that came to many of them upon foreign soil. The naval and Veterans' Bureau hospitals shelter many of those young men who went forth in the full prowess of physical health and who returned to die slowly here at home. Many were saved from either of these two destinies, and of that number some are here on this floor today. I know the decision they will make when they are confronted with the choice of keeping our ships at home or sending millions of our youths to defend the rights of merchant ships who venture into belligerent zones.

I, for one, reiterate my previous statement that I will vote for the act which prohibits American vessels from entering areas of danger, which prohibits American vessels from bringing danger to America.

And I have the heartfelt conviction that this act providing for cash and carry will enable our Nation to be, at least, as neutral as she is today.

Of course, it is true that one who speaks of "neutrality" expresses his own definition thereof.

The present law is commonly referred to as the neutrality law; yet that law unquestionably favors one of the belligerents in the present war.

Mr. Speaker, in an aggressive war there can no longer be neutrality. We must stand with the nation that keeps its word, and we must not side, even indirectly, with a nation that, through temper, through ambition, through wrong belief, or for any one of a hundred reasons, violates its pledge and proceeds once again to bring down upon us such an avalanche as 1914 let loose.

In looking at Europe today, do we find any of those nations of such sterling character, with such clean hands as America would be proud to grasp in friendship? History answeres this with an emphatic "No," and every signpost indicating the upbuilding of America tells us to keep out of Europe.

It is said that repeal of the embargo and enactment of legislation providing for cash and carry will result in our giving aid and comfort to Great Britain and her Allies.

Mr. Speaker, as an American, as a militant advocate of democracy and a Member of this Congress, I wish to state that I have no desire to plead the cause of the British Empire, which has inflicted a cruel, barbarous, and savage reign of terror upon its unwilling subjects throughout the world, whether they were Irish or Arabian, Jewish or Indian, Egyptian or African. The record of the growth of the British Empire is an unhappy, a shameless tale of aggression.

England has maintained a symbol of democracy on the isles of Britain and Scotland -- Scotland was acquired by union and not by conquest -- but the guaranties of the British Constitution have been confined strictly to those subjects of the British Crown who dwelt on the two favored isles.

It should be recalled that in 1844, on the occasion of Lord John Russell's motion in the House of Commons to inqure into the condition in Ireland, Lord Macaulay said:

You admit that you govern Ireland not as you govern England, not as you govern Scotland, but as you govern your new conquest in Scinde; not by means of the respect which the people feel for the law, but by means of bayonets and artillery and intrenched camps.

No wonder that as an American my sympathies have never been, and are not now with that British Government which, in the words of the martyred Robert Emmet, is a Government steeled to barbarity by the cries of the orphans and the tears of the widows it has made. Ever since the British invader entered the glorious island of Erin in 1172 and took from the Irish people the lands of their ancestors, the story of English dominion has been written in fire and blood.

The Irish Nation was wrongfully and viciously deprived of its inheritance in that early time. Not content with this outrage, British soldiers drove the people from their homes, and confiscated every farm and every cottage, until in 1611 the Irish were driven from their hearths to find refuge by the roadside or in the hidden mountain caves. But the British soldiers lacked the industry and the skill to till the soil they had stolen, and so gradually the natives of Ireland were permitted to return to those farms to work them almost as serfs. When they had reclaimed many of these farms from the bogs, when the dairies in the Irish hills were once more bright with pans of cream, English absentee landlords demanded enormous rents, with the only alternative, eviction. From 1760 to 1800, the people of Ireland were again maintaining themselves -- from their farms, their dairies, their industries. They were self-supporting during those 40 years when the population was twice as great as it is today. Then in 1800 the mailed fist of the British conqueror showed itself again in the act of union, of which Daniel O'Connell said:

I admit there is the force of a law, because it has been supported by the policeman's truncheon, by the soldier's bayonet, and by the horseman's sword, because it is supported by the courts of law and those who have power to adjudicate in them; but I say, solemnly, it is not supported by constitutional right.

No, my friends; the union was begot in iniquity; it was perpetrated in fraud and cruelty. It was no compact, no bargain, but it was an act of the most decided tyranny and corruption that was ever yet perpetrated. Trial by jury was suspended, the right of personal protection was at an end, courts martial sat throughout the land, and the county of Kildare, among others, flowed with blood.

The Green Isle did indeed flow with blood, with the blood of gallant, nay, heroic, Irishmen like Robert Emmet, who died in 1803, whose last plea was for the "emancipation of my country from the superhuman oppression under which she has so long and too patiently travailed." His last protest was against "the yoke of a foreign and unrelenting tyranny."

His protest found his persecutors deaf, and still determined to torture these innocent victims of aggression. One of the most disgraceful periods in the Irish persecution followed shortly. In 1847 came the famine, when 2,000,000 died, when the inhumanity of Britain to Irishmen set a new standard of savagery. Gilbert K. Chesterton, an Englishman born and bred, has described it thus:

The conduct of the English toward the Irish after the rebellion was quite simply the conduct of one man who traps and binds another and then calmly cuts him about with a knife. The conduct during the famine was quite simply the conduct of the first man if he entertained the later moments of the second man by remarking in a chatty manner on the very hopeful chances of his bleeding to death. The British Prime Minister publicly refused to stop the famine by the use of English ships. The British Prime Minister positively spread the famine by making the half-starved population of Ireland pay for the starved ones. The common verdict of a coroner's jury upon some emaciated wretch was "willful murder by Lord John Russell."

And that verdict was not only the verdict of Irish public opinion but is the verdict of history -- The Crimes of England.

It is not surprising that the men of Ireland became convinced that they could guarantee economic security and cultural opportunity to their children only by freeing themselves from the chains of oppression. Eighteen hundred and sixty-seven saw the Fenians organizing for a free Ireland -- and the English soldiery brutally overcoming them. Independence was the prayer of the Irishman. But England, that vaunted democracy, not only failed to heed the plea but ground her heel in contempt upon her Irish subjects. Bullets and destruction formed her answer.

By every peaceful means during the succeeding years Ireland sought liberty. And each succeeding decade saw Ireland more enslaved and more impoverished, until in 1916 came the Easter Rebellion of that group of ardent young patriots led by Padraic Pearse, and the eyes of the world were suddenly focused on the small island where the most brutal atrocities were being perpetrated by the Black and Tans, composed partly of convicts sent by Britain.

In 1918, following the principle of self-determination of small nations enunciated by our great and now deceased President, Woodrow Wilson, the Irish people held a general election under British law on the question whether to remain in the Empire or to establish a free and independent government of their own. Eighty percent of the entire voting population of the country voted for an independent government, free from the Empire, and proceeded to establish such a government, which has never been dissolved.

Nevertheless, in the latter part of 1921, after continued fighting for recognition of this lawful government, which was functioning successfully even in its law courts, a truce was arranged, and at a conference in London the Irish representatives were delivered the ultimatum of England, namely, the partition of Ireland and dominion status or the alternative of immediate and terrible war.

Even today the cry for independence is heard, and will continue to be heard until Ireland is as free as Cuba.

Our own experience with England in the light of history has been a most unhappy one. It might be well to refresh the recollection of those whose memories have become somewhat clouded by the interval of time since the World War with the fact that those in high places in the British Government have on repeated occasions offered only gross insults to the United States in recognition of American aid to the Allies of the last World War in men, money, and supplies. The English response to any request for payment of war debts has been derisively to salute the United States as Uncle Shylock.

I cannot agree with those who would place this legislation on the basis of war or no war. It is my belief that the United States can formulate a foreign policy which is characteristically American and which will safeguard American interests and American ideals in all parts of the world, without fear or favor of any nation or group of nations.

I have every confidence in President Roosevelt's foreign policy and in his determination to guard American interests and to prevent American manhood from leaving our shores to take part in the present war.

With that conviction, I am prepared to vote in favor of the act now under consideration. (Applause.)

EDITORIAL -- THE U.S. REPUBLIC FOREVER.

Source: The Gaelic American, New York City, December 13, 1941.

The Republic of the United States has been subjected to a dastardly attack. The . . . Japanese Empire has stabbed us in the back. Congress has spoken. While we opposed war, we abide by the decision of the Congress. The time to close ranks has arrived. The American Irish, as always, support the Republic.

The GAELIC AMERICAN had hoped that our beloved United States would be saved from the horrors of the war which is devastating Europe. It has week after week pointed out the powerful influence of British propaganda to get this country involved on her side . . . . From the moment when Japan dropped her first bomb on December 7, 1941, we aligned ourselves unreservedly behind the Government, as our race has done in every crisis in the Nation's history, from the Revolution and the War of 1812 to the Civil War, the War with Spain, and World War No. 1. Irish blood has been poured out freely on every battlefield where the honor and interests of the United States were at stake, and that proud record will be maintained untarnished now and in the future . . . .

No more today than at any time in the existence of this Republic, can any question be raised of our loyalty and fidelity. True, we have supported the people and Government of Ireland in their decision to remain strictly neutral. This decision has the undivided support of the entire Irish nation. In justice and fairness to the people and Government of Ireland, we hope that the American people and Government will respect their neutrality and not coerce Eire into a position which in all probability would wipe out the last remnant of the race in the old land.

As far as we of Irish blood in America are concerned, it is hardly necessary to say that in America's hour of need, every Irish man and woman, from one end of the country to the other, will stand by the flag and the Constitution and by the Country, as men of Irish blood have done for generations. Our allegiance is directed to only one thing -- the Stars and Stripes of America.

ONWARD TO VICTORY.

IRISH IMMIGRATION ADVERSELY AFFECTED BY THE IMMIGRATION AND NATIONALITY ACT OF 1965

Source: <u>Congressional Record</u>, vol. 113, pt. 10, pp. 13166-8 (Remarks in House of Representatives by Rep. W. F. Ryan of New York).

Mr. Speaker, when Congress passed the Immigration and Nationality Act of 1965 it was thought to be a major advancement toward facilitating immigration to the country. . . . However . . . the new section 212 (a) (14) has had severe effects on immigration . . . particularly Irish Immigration. . . .

Applications for visas have seriously declined. In 1964 there were 5,817 applications; in 1965 there were 4,750; and in 1966 only 1,996. . . . Prospective applicants were discouraged once they knew of the new section 212 (a) (14). The number of visas actually issued has also taken a sharp decline. . . .

There is no doubt that section 212 (a) (14) has caused a decrease in Irish immigration to the United States. As many Irish visa applicants are unskilled or semiskilled workers, they are unable to qualify. . . .

Earlier this year I introduced H. R. 7775 to rectify this situation by removing the inequity of section 212 (a) (14). . . . It is an inequity which particularly affects Irish immigration. I know that because of our distinguished Speaker and the late President Kennedy as well as several members of the Congress who are of Irish descent, I need not dwell on the magnificent contribution of the Irish to our Nation. It would be to America's detriment to continue 212 (a) (14) in its present form. The law should be changed and changed quickly.

EXTRACT FROM SPEECH BY SENATOR EDWARD M. KENNEDY OF MASSACHUSETTS IN U. S. SENATE, OCTOBER 20, 1971.

Source: Congressional Record, vol. 117, no. 157 (October 20, 1971): Senate.

Mr. President, I am pleased to join with Senator Abraham Ribicoff in introducing a Senate resolution calling for the immediate withdrawal of British troops from Northern Ireland and the establishment of a united Ireland. An identical resolution is being introduced today in the House of Representatives by Congressman Hugh Carey of Brooklyn.

We believe that the resolution states the only realistic means to end the killing in Northern Ireland and to bring peace to a land that has given so much to America, a land that has done so much to enrich the history of our own Nation, a land that is suffering so deeply today.

The conscience of America cannot keep silent when men and women of Ireland are dying. Britian has lost its way, and the innocent people of Northern Ireland are now the ones who must suffer. The time has come for Americans of every faith and political persuasion to speak out. We owe ourselves and our sacred heritage no less.

Down through the centuries, the people of Ireland have been forced to wage a continuing and arduous struggle for freedom and equality. For generations, division and despair have scarred the countryside. The ancient right of self-determination has been denied. Often alone, often without notice from others throughout the world, brave men and women of Ireland have given their lives for the principles they hold dear. Millions have been driven from their homes, forced to leave the land they love, obliged to seek a new life in nations where the yoke of repression could not reach.

Today the Irish struggle again. But now they are not alone. They have the support of free peoples in every corner of the world. Their cause is just, and the reforms they seek are basic to all democracies worthy of the name . . . .

The explosive situation in Northern Ireland transcends the traditional feeling of those who believe that America ought not to intervene in the affairs of another nation. That principle is utterly without application here. There are ties between America and Ireland that simply cannot be ignored.

As President Kennedy liked to say, America is a nation of immigrants. The Irish yield to none in their contributions to the people and culture of America. The waves of Irish immigrants who sought our shores in the 19th century launched a movement that spanned our continent and changed the course of American history. They say today that Irish blood flows in the veins of one out of every seven Ameeicans. There are more Irishmen in America now than in the Ireland they left behind.

The Irish have had a monumental impact on the America we know today. Wherever we look--in business and the labor movement, in literature and music, in science and religion--and above all in public service at every level of government, we find citizens of Irish descent who helped to make our Nation great.

They built our railroads, dug our coal, erected our buildings and our churches. They organized our unions and our businesses. They fought in all our wars. They gave us giants like Eugene O'Neill and Scott Fitzgerald in the world of literature and drama; Louis Sullivan in architecture; George M. Cohan and Victor Herbert in the field of music; actresses like Helen Hayes; athletes like John L. Sullivan and Gene Tunney, John McGraw and Connie Mack; pillars of the Church like Archbishop Ireland, Cardinal Gibbons, Cardinal Spellman, and Cardinal Cushing; labor leaders like George Meany; military heroes from the Revolution to Vietnam; and political leaders at every level--Federal, State, and local--whose dedication helped ensure the growth and stability of our Nation.

But the wearing of the green knows no narrow boundary of religion or nationality. Even without these bonds of blood and history, the deepening tragedy of Ulster today would demand that voices of concerned Americans everywhere be raised against the killing and violence of Northern Ireland, just as we seek an end to brutality and repression everywhere. But, because the killing and the violence go on in Ireland, the call to action in America is irresistible . . . .

A PLEA FOR AMERICAN INVOLVEMENT, 1972.

Source: Newsletter of the American Committee for Ulster Justice, June 1, 1972.

The United States Role in the Irish Question

Channel 13's public forum T. V. program "The Advocates" recently debated the motion 'that the United States should support the unification of Ireland.' The format was such that counsel for and against the proposition questioned outstanding spokesmen of the major parties to the conflict in Northern Ireland. The television audience was invited to vote for or against the motion by mailing their ballots to the T. V. station. The result of the ballot showed the American public overwhelmingly in favor of support for the unification of Ireland as 77% of the more than 15,000 votes cast were affirmative.

There are many reasons why the people of the United States and the government should be interested in helping to find a solution to the present conflict in Northern Ireland. The following presents some of the reasons, but fundamentally the U. S. must interest itself on the grounds of kinship, our own colonial past and the fact that the presence of violence anywhere is a festering sore that has a habit in these days of instant communication of spreading.

On the grounds of kinship, there are as many as 40,000,000 Americans whose ancestors (one or more of them) came from Ireland. Some twelve of the United States Presidents have had Irish ancestors including Presidents Kennedy and Nixon. The contribution of the Irish and their descendants to the building of this great nation is a story fully documented and well known to the American people. In the case of the affinity of the U. S. with the State of Israel many specific economic, military and diplomatic steps have been taken to aid and support her in times of danger. The plight of the Jewish community in the Soviet Union, surely by other yardsticks of measurement an internal matter for the Moscow authorities to resolve, is a topic of discussion in President Nixon's trip to the Kremlin. The State Department has apparently overlooked the argument in this case that the matter of the Jewish community is a domestic affair of the Soviet Union. Are not the grounds of kinship as strong in the case of Ireland as in the case of Israel?

The violence in N. I. is the final chapter in Ireland's seemingly eternal struggle against British colonialism. The United States, which itself was the first colony of Britain to successfully initiate its independence, must look with sympathy on the fight of the people who of all the nations on earth are most identified with the historical movement of national liberation and political independence. Benjamin Franklin understood the position of the Irish people and when he addressed the Irish Parliament soliciting their aid he received their wholehearted support for the enterprise then astir in England's North American colonies. Five thousand of General Washington's troops were Irish, including three of his Generals.

Ireland inspired the downfall of the greatest colonial empire ever created. Does she not have the right to the sympathy and concern of those she helped liberate from the same cruel yoke?

The United States has interceded in one way or another, without the involvement of troops in many disputes between states in recent years. President Nixon has sent Secretary of State Rogers to find some basis for agreement and the lessening of tensions in the Middle East. President Johnson sent Cyrus Vance to mediate in the Cyprus crisis and his Assistant Secretary of State for Latin America mediated between Great Britain and Honduras in 1964 after both nations broke off diplomatic relations over the question of British Honduras.

While the United States is maintaining at great cost, a large standing army in Europe under our committment to NATO, the British Army has more than 15,500 of its Army personnel, not to mention all of its intelligence and other services, concentrated in the colonial war in Northern Ireland. A recent edition of the London Economist recognized that such a development has seriously undermined Great Britain's commitment to its NATO allies.

The United States need not involve itself in any military solution in Northern Ireland, but rather the influence of friendly persuasion should be used to convince the United Kingdom that the only permanent solution lies in a Free, United and Independent Ireland.

STATISTICAL TABLES

The material on Irish-American immigration and population trends contained in the following tables is drawn from: (a) U. S. Immigration and Naturalization Service, Annual Reports; (b) U. S. Dept. of Commerce, Bureau of the Census, Census Reports; (c) U. S. Government Printing Office, Historical Statistics, Colonial Times to 1957 (1957, and Supplement, 1962); (d) U. S. Immigration Commission, Reports, III (U. S. Doc. 5878, No. 756: Statistical Review of Immigration, 1820-1910); (e) N. Y. S. Commission of Emigration, Report, 1871 (U. S. Doc. 1470, No. 1); (f) His Majesty's Stationery Office, Census of Ireland, 1901: Pt. II, General Report (1901); (g) Ministry of Social Welfare, Ireland, Report of Commission on Emigration and Other Population Problems (1954).

EMIGRANTS FROM IRELAND TO THE UNITED STATES DURING THE NINETEENTH CENTURY

Aside from the years 1800-1802, when a brief interval of peace and a simultaneous decline in the Ulster linen industry combined to stimulate an annual emigration of about 6,000, relatively few Irish came to the U. S. during the Napoleonic Wars, and practically none in 1812-14, when Britain and the U. S. were at war with one another. There were approximately 1,500 emigrants in 1815, and increasingly large numbers during the next five years. Reasonably accurate (though by no means definitive) figures are available from 1820 on.

Year	Emigrants	Year	Emigrants
1820	3,614	1854	111,095
1821	1,518	1855	57,164
1822	2,267	1856	58,777
1823	1,908	1857	66,080
1824	2,345	1858	31,498
1825	4,826	1859	41,180
1826	4,821	1860	52,103
1827	9,772	1861	28,209
1828	7,861	1862	33,521
1829	9,995	1863	94,477
1830	12,765	1864	94,368
1831	13,598	1865	82,085
1832	15,092	1866	86,594
1833	14,177	1867	79,571
1834	16,928	1868	57,662
1835	13,307	1869	66,467
1836	15,000	1870	67,891
1837	22,089	1871	65,591
1838	8,149	1872	66,752
1839	20,790	1873	75,536
1840	25,957	1874	48,136
1841	36,428	1875	31,433
1842	49,920	1876	16,432
1843	23,597	1877	13,991
1844	37,569	1878	18,602
1845	50,207	1879	30,058
1846	68,023	1880	83,018
1847	118,120	1881	67,339
1848	151,003	1882	68,300
1849	180,189	1883	82,849
1850	184,351	1884	59,204
1851	219,232	1885	50,657
1852	195,801	1886	52,858
1853	156,970	1887	69,084

1888	66,306	1896	39,952
1890	52,110	1897	32,822
1891	53,438	1898	30,878
1892	48,966	1899	38,631
1893	42,122	1900	41,848
1894	39,597	1901	35,535
1895	52,027		

NOTE: Figures do not include Irishmen entering the U. S. from Great Britain, who formed a significant proportion of the "British" listings in U. S. immigration records, or those who entered (legally or illegally) through Canada.

DECLINE IN THE POPULATION OF IRELAND DURING THE PERIOD OF HEAVIEST EMIGRATION

YEAR	POPULATION	RATE OF DECREASE IN DECADE
1841	8,196,597	
1851	6,574,278	19.85%
1861	5,888,564	11.50%
1871	5,412,377	6.67%
1881	5,174,836	4.39%
1891	4,704,750	9.08%
1901	4,456,546	5.23%

As of 1970, the estimated population of Ireland (Republic and Northern Ireland) was 4,468,000.

IRISH-BORN POPULATION OF PRINCIPAL U. S. CITIES IN 1870, AFTER THE GREAT MID-NINETEENTH CENTURY WAVE OF IMMIGRATION.

CITY	TOTAL POPULATION	IRISH-BORN
New York, N. Y.	942,292	202,000
Philadelphia, Pa.	674,022	96,698
Brooklyn, N. Y.	376,099	73,986
St. Louis, Mo.	310,864	32,239
Chicago, Ill.	298,977	40,000
Baltimore, Md.	267,354	15,223
Boston, Mass.	250,526	56,000
Cincinnati, Ohio	216,239	18,624
New Orleans, La.	191,418	14,693
San Francisco, Cal.	149,473	25,864
Buffalo, N. Y.	117,714	11,264
Washington, D. C.	109,200	6,948
Newark, N. J.	105,059	12,481
Louisville, Ky.	100,753	7,626
Cleveland, Ohio	92,829	9,964
Pittsburgh, Pa.	86,076	13,119
Jersey City, N. J.	82,546	17,665
Detroit, Mich.	79,577	6,970
Milwaukee, Wis.	71,440	3,784
Albany, N. Y.	69,422	13,276
Providence, R. I.	68,904	12,085
Rochester, N. Y.	62,386	6,078
Allegheny, Pa.	53,180	4,034
Richmond, Va.	51,038	1,239
New Haven, Conn.	50,840	9,601

The total population of the United States in 1870 was 38,558,371, of whom 1,855,827 were born in Ireland. One-half of the Irish-born population resided in the three states of New York, Pennsylvania, and Massachusetts. These three, plus New Jersey and the other five New England states, accounted for two-thirds of all Irish-born residents.

EMIGRANTS FROM IRELAND TO THE UNITED STATES DURING THE TWENTIETH CENTURY

Year	Emigrants	Year	Emigrants
1901	35,535	1936	444
1902	29,138	1937	531
1903	35,310	1938	1,085
1904	36,142	1939	1,189
1905	52,945	1940	839
1906	34,995	1941	272
1907	34,530	1942	83
1908	30,556	1943	165
1909	25,033	1944	112
1910	29,855	1945	427
1911	29,112	1946	1,816
1912	25,879	1947	2,574
1913	27,876	1948	7,534
1914	24,688	1949	8,678
1915	14,185	1950	5,842
1916	8,639	1951	3,144
1917	5,406	1952	3,526
1918	331	1953	4,304
1919	474	1954	4,655
1920	9,591	1955	5,222
1921	28,435	1956	5,607
1922	10,579	1957	8,227
1923	15,740	1958	9,134
1924	17,111	1959	6,595
1925	26,650	1960	6,918
1926	24,897	1961	5,738
1927	28,545	1962	5,118
1928	25,268	1963	5,000
1929	19,921	1964	5,200
1930	23,445	1965	5,463
1931	7,305	1966	4,700
1932	539	1967	1,901
1933	338	1968	2,268
1934	443	1969	1,989
1935	454	1970	1,562

Fluctuations in the number of immigrants, and the marked decline in annual admissions during the period since 1930 reflect wartime interruption of overseas traffic, changing domestic conditions in Ireland, and the limitations imposed by the Immigration Acts of 1924-9 and 1952 which set quotas successively decreasing from 28,567 to 17,756.

THE IRISH SHARE OF AMERICAN IMMIGRATION

DECADE	ALL IMMIGRANTS	IRISH
1820-30	151,824	54,338
1831-40	599,125	207,381
1841-50	1,713,251	780,719
1851-60	2,598,214	914,119
1861-70	2,314,824	435,778
1871-80	2,812,191	436,871
1881-90	5,246,613	655,482
1891-1900	3,687,564	390,179
1901-10	8,795,386	339,065
1911-20	5,735,811	146,181
1921-30	4,107,209	220,591
1931-40	528,431	13,167
1941-50	1,035,039	25,377
1951-60	2,515,479	57,332
1961-70	3,321,777	37,461
TOT. 1820-1970	45,162,638	4,713,868 (10.4%)

The Irish constituted 42.3% of all immigrants between 1820 and 1850, and 35.2% of those coming between 1851 and 1860. Thereafter, the percentage declined steadily, to 18.8% in 1861-70, 15.5% in 1871-80, 12.5% in 1881-90, and 10.6% in 1891-1900. During 1961-70, the Irish accounted for only 1.1% of all immigrants.

THE IRISH ELEMENT IN THE POPULATION OF THE UNITED STATES

YEAR	TOTAL POPULATION	IRISH-BORN POPULATION
1850	23,191,876	961,719 (4.15%
1860	31,443,321	1,611,304 (5.12%)
1870	38,558,371	1,855,827 (4.81%)
1880	50,155,783	1,854,571 (3.70%)
1890	62,622,250	1,871,509 (2.80%)
1900	75,568,686	1,615,459 (2.13%)
1910	91,972,266	1,352,155
1920	105,710,620	1,037,233
1930	122,775,646	923,642
1940	131,669,275	678,447
1950	150,697,361	520,359
1960	179,323,175	406,433
1970	203,184,772	277,000

Native-born Americans with one or both parents Irish-born:

1910	3,304,015	1950	1,921,385
1920	3,122,013	1960	1,619,446
1930	2,858,897	1970	1,300,000 (est.)
1940	2,109,740		

THE U. S. CENSUS FOR 1970 LISTED 13,282,000 AMERICANS (6.7% OF THE TOTAL POPULATION) AS BEING OF IRISH ANCESTRY.

BIBLIOGRAPHY

The principle of utility, rather than that of comprehensiveness, has guided the selection of the following titles. Along with numerous works dedicated to the exaltation or execration of the Irish, which are of dubious historical value, all but a small sampling of the many excellent studies devoted to local or regional Irish-American activities have been omitted. The journals of the various state and municipal historical societies may be consulted, with profit, for material of this sort. Biographies and memoirs of notable Irish-Americans have been included only where they seemed to offer insight into the general experience of the Irish-American community.

THE IRISH BACKGROUND

Arensberg, Conrad, The Irish Countryman: An Anthropological Study, New York, 1937.

Beckett, J. C., The Making of Modern Ireland, 1603-1923, London, 1966.

Coogan, Timothy Patrick, Ireland Since the Rising, London, 1966.

Cullen, L. M., Life in Ireland, New York, 1968.

McCaffrey, Lawrence J., The Irish Question, 1800-1922, Lexington, Ky., 1968.

Moody, T. W. and Martin, F. X., The Course of Irish History, New York, 1969.

THE IRISH IN AMERICA: GENERAL STUDIES

Calkin, H. L., "The United States Government and the Irish," Irish Historical Studies, IX (Mar. 1954), 28-52.

Crimmins, J. D., Irish American Historical Miscellany, New York, 1905.

Duff, John B., The Irish in the United States, Belmont, Cal., 1971.

Jones, Maldwyn A., American Immigration, Chicago, 1960.

Potter, George W., To the Golden Door. The Story of the Irish in Ireland and America, Boston, 1960.

Shannon, William V., The American Irish, New York, 1963.

Wittke, Carl, The Irish in America, Baton Rouge, La., 1956.

THE IRISH IN AMERICA: COLONIAL AND EARLY NATIONAL PERIOD

Adams, William F., Ireland and Irish Emigration to the New World from 1815 to the Famine, New Haven, 1932.

Beckett, J. C., Protestant Dissent in Ireland, 1687-1780, London, 1948.

Dickson, R. J., Ulster Emigration to Colonial America, 1718-1775, London, 1966.

Dunaway, W. F., The Scotch-Irish of Colonial Pennsylvania, Chapel Hill, N. C., 1944.

McGee, Thomas D'Arcy, History of the Irish Settlers in North America, New York, 1852.

Maginniss, T. H., The Irish Contribution to America's Independence, Philadelphia, 1913.

Maguire, J. F., The Irish in America, London, 1868.

Moody, T. W., "Irish and Scotch-Irish in Eighteenth-Century America," Studies, XXXV (1946), 123-140.

----- "The Ulster Scot in Colonial and Revolutionary America," Studies, XXXIV (1945), 52-69.

Myers, A. C., Immigration of the Irish Quakers into Pennsylvania, 1692-1750, Swarthmore, Pa., 1902.

O'Brien, George, The Economic History of Ireland from the Union to the Famine, London, 1914.

O'Brien, Michael J., George Washington's Associations with the Irish, New York, 1937.

----- A Hidden Phase of American History: Ireland's Part in America's Struggle for Liberty, New York, 1919.

----- Pioneer Irish in New England, New York, 1937.

----- The Irish at Bunker Hill, Shannon, 1968.

Purcell, Richard J., "The Irish Contribution to Colonial New York," Studies, XXVII (1928), 41-60.

Smith, A. E., Colonists in Bondage: White Servitude and Convict Labor in America, 1607-1776, Chapel Hill, N. C., 1947.

THE IRISH IN AMERICA: SINCE THE FAMINE

Bagenal, P. H., The American Irish and Their Influence on Irish Politics, London, 1882.

Brown, Thomas N., Irish-American Nationalism, 1870-1890, Philadelphia, 1966.

Byrne, Stephen, Irish Emigration to the United States, New York, 1873.

Cuddy, Edward, "Irish-American Propagandists and American Neutrality, 1914-1917," MidAmerica, v. 49. no. 4 (October, 1967), 252-75.

D'Arcy, William, The Fenian Movement in the United States, 1858-1886, Washington, D. C., 1947.

Green, James J., "American Catholics and the Irish Land League, 1879-1822," Catholic Historical Review, XXXV (Apr. 1949), 19-42.

Levine, E. M., The Irish and Irish Politicians, Notre Dame, Ind., 1966.

Lonn, Ella, Foreigners in the Confederacy, Chapel Hill, N. C., 1940.

----- Foreigners in the Union Army and Navy, Baton Rouge, La. , 1951.

MacDonagh, Oliver, "Irish Emigration to the United States of America and the British Colonies during the Famine," in R. Dudley Edwards and T. Desmond Williams, eds., The Great Famine, Studies in Irish History, 1845-52, New York, 1957.

O'Grady, John "Irish Colonization in the United States," Studies, XIX (1930), 387-407.

Roberts, E. F., Ireland in America, New York, 1931.

Schrier, Arnold, Ireland and the American Emigration, 1850-1900, Minneapolis, 1958.

Tansill, C. C., America and the Fight for Irish Freedom, 1866-1922, New York, 1957.

Ward, Alan J., Ireland and Anglo-American Relations, 1899-1921, London, 1969.

Woodham-Smith, C., The Great Hunger. Ireland, 1845-1849, New York, 1962.

THE IRISH IN AMERICA: PARTICULAR INDIVIDUALS AND TOPICS

Ahearn, Robert G., Thomas Francis Meagher. An Irish Revolutionary in America, Boulder, Colo., 1949.

Broehl, W. G., The Molly Maguires, Cambridge, Mass., 1964.

Browne, Henry J., The Catholic Church and the Knights of Labor, Washington, D. C., 1949.

Burns, James M., John F. Kennedy. A Political Profile, New York, 1960.

Devoy, John, Recollections of an Irish Rebel, New York, 1929.

Ellis, Elmer, Mr. Dooley's America, New York, 1941.

Ellis, John T., The Life of James Cardinal Gibbons, 2 vols., New York, 1952.

Emmet, Thomas A., Incidents of My Life, New York, 1911.

Gibson, Florence E., Attitudes of the New York Irish Toward State and National Affairs, 1848-1892, New York, 1951.

Glazer, Nathan, and Moynihan, Daniel P., Beyond the Melting Pot, Cambridge, Mass., 1959.

Gurn, Joseph, Charles Carroll of Carrollton, New York, 1932.

Hackett, James D., Bishops of the United States of Irish Birth or Descent, New York, 1936.

Hanchett, William, Irish: Charles G. Halpine in Civil War America, Syracuse, 1970.

Handlin, Oscar, Boston's Immigrants, Rev. and enl. ed., Cambridge, Mass., 1959.

Jones, Paul, The Irish Brigade, New York, 1969.

McCartan, Patrick, With DeValera in America, Dublin, 1932.

Man, Albon P., "The Irish in New York in the Early Eighteen-Sixties," Irish Historical Studies, VII (Sept. 1950), 87-108.

Murphy, Robert C., and Mannion, Lawrence J., The History of the Society of the Friendly Sons of Saint Patrick in the City of New York, 1784-to 1955, New York, 1962.

Niehaus, E. F., The Irish in New Orleans, 1800-1860, Baton Rouge, La., 1965.

Oberste, W. H., Texas Irish Empresarios and their Colonies, Austin, 1953.

O'Brien, William, and Ryan, Desmond, ed., Devoy's Post Bag, 1871-1928. 2 vols., Dublin, 1948-53.

O'Dea, John, History of the Ancient Order of Hibernians. . . ., 4 vols., Philadelphia, 1923.

Phelan, Josephine, The Ardent Exile. The Life and Times of D'Arcy McGee, Toronto, 1951.

Pratt, Julius W., "John L. O'Sullivan and Manifest Destiny," New York History, XIV (1933), 213-34.

Purcell, Richard J., "The New York Commissioners of Emigration and Irish Immigrants, 1847-1860," Studies, XXXVII (1948), 29-42.

Riordan, William, Plunkitt of Tammany Hall, New York, 1963.

Rowley, William E., "The Irish Aristocracy of Albany, 1798-1878," New York History, LII (1971), 275-304.

Walsh, Louis J., John Mitchel, London, 1934.

THE IRISH IN AMERICA: OTHER SOURCES OF INFORMATION

The American Irish Historical Society (991 Fifth Avenue, New York, N. Y.) maintains a large reference and research library dedicated to Irish and Irish-American history. In addition, its Journal, published annually 1897 to 1931, and its Recorder, published annually since then, contain a wealth of historical articles and data. Its educational mission is furthered through a continuing program of lectures and exhibitions.

The American Committee for Irish Studies, with its membership drawn mainly from the academic world, is primarily concerned with Irish, rather than Irish-American, topics, but its annual conferences occasionally touch on American themes. It elects new officers each year, and has no permanent headquarters.

The Irish American Cultural Institute (683 Osceola Ave., St. Paul, Minn.) publishes a monthly newsletter, Ducas, that "explores the cultural heritage of Americans of Irish ancestry," and Eire-Ireland, a quarterly devoted to Irish studies.

Irish-American newspapers, which flourished in great profusion during the heyday of immigration, have declined in number. The principal survivors--all published in New York City--are The Irish World, The Advocate, and The Echo, all of which carry news of Irish-American social, cultural, and sporting events in New York and other parts of the country, as well as maintaining a regular coverage of developments in Ireland.

INDEX